"Few writers can pull off the r
this book. Tiffany Kriner's voice
perceptive, erudite yet conversational. With humane reflections
that reckon with James Baldwin's haunting voice and the para-
doxes and travails of academia, family, and farming, this book is
genuinely remarkable and gloriously undefinable. Consider it a
seed that will bear life-giving fruit in all those who, with patience,
attend to its pages."

—Claude Atcho
pastor of Church of the Resurrection in Charlottesville, VA,
and author of *Reading Black Books*

"A farm, writes Tiffany Kriner, is a 'field full of powers and forces,'
and so are her paragraphs. In this beautifully written book, she
turns the clichés of an evangelical childhood into a robust adult
faith, the fragments of American history into a story of repentance and renewal, and a beat-up bit of land into a life-giving farm.
She looks at so many things—at owls; at the writings of Chesnutt,
Whitman, and Baldwin; at armed, possibly dangerous neighbors—
with a generous, transforming attention."

—Phil Christman
author of *Midwest Futures*

"Kriner is fearless in her exploration of the difficulty of place
and land in a peripatetic and racially scarred America. Here are
shades of Wendell Berry, Annie Dillard, and Julian of Norwich,
but *In Thought, Word, and Seed* has, first, a voice all its own. Lu-
minous. Audacious. Holy."

—Beth Felker Jones
professor of theology, Northern Seminary

"*In Thought, Word, and Seed* blends honest reflection on some of today's hardest issues with scenes of earth and sky. It's thoughtfully considered and beautifully written."

—Nurya Love Parish
executive director of Plainsong Farm in Rockford, MI, and author of *Resurrection Matters: Church Renewal for Creation's Sake*

"I love the smorgasbord of genres powering this collection—the letter, the litany, reports from the field—all in service of questions vital to the moment: how to care for those with whom we share the earth; how to confront one's racial innocence; and how to repair the ecosystems, both public and internal, that have been 'laid waste.' Tiffany Kriner trusts soul-sustaining and soul-wrenching farm work, community reckoning, and relationship building—the precious and challenging tasks that make up her days—to create occasions for the authentic encounters she seeks. And, because her writing is wise and beautiful, in seeking she quickly becomes a trusted guide. How to approach the overgrown, the neglected, the seemingly hopeless forces out there? Kriner's method of response—'I sharpen my loppers and pray for everything'—is perfect for our fraught and tender era."

—Lia Purpura
author of *All the Fierce Tethers*

"In this lovely mash-up of literary criticism, theology, prayer, and memoir, Tiffany Eberle Kriner invites us into the joyful, frustrating, sweat-inducing, painfully exasperating, and satisfying work of redemption with the land. This is a deeply grounded, wisely attentive, and beautifully allusive book. A wonderful read that will invite you to come back for a second (or third) visit."

—Brian Walsh
farmer at Russet House Farm in Ontario and coauthor of *Beyond Homelessness*

In Thought, Word, and Seed

Reckonings from a Midwest Farm

Tiffany Eberle Kriner

WILLIAM B. EERDMANS PUBLISHING COMPANY
GRAND RAPIDS, MICHIGAN

Wm. B. Eerdmans Publishing Co.
4035 Park East Court SE, Grand Rapids, Michigan 49546
www.eerdmans.com

29 28 27 26 25 24 23   1 2 3 4 5 6 7

ISBN 978-0-8028-8290-5

Library of Congress Cataloging-in-Publication Data

A catalog record for this book is available from the Library
of Congress.

Unless otherwise noted, Scripture quotations are from the
New Revised Standard Version of the Bible.

Permissions to reprint materials used in this book are ac-
knowledged on pp. 197–98.

Contents

Foreword

The five lyric essays that make up Tiffany Eberle Kriner's *In Thought, Word, and Seed* trace a series of reflections that arise as she and her husband purchase sixty worn acres in northern Illinois and begin the work of restoring or redeeming—healing, she says at one point—the land. Like Thoreau in *Walden*, or like those who have carried on his work (Annie Dillard in *Holy the Firm*, James Galvin in *The Meadow*, Kathleen Norris in *Dakota*), Kriner's work roots itself in a specific place and time and attempts to lift its particulars up into meaning and vision and praise. The couple's name for their enterprise, Root and Sky Farm, reflects this earthbound, upward motion. This is no simple thing, of course, and much of the work of these striking essays, like much of the work on the farm, is spent in clearing pathways, uncovering histories, and facing what has been hidden away, all, as Fanny Howe puts it, in the name of actually "understanding your own condition." Think of these essays as spiritual improvisations, peering deep into the particulars of place and soul, swinging back and forth from one to the other, and slowly being broken and transformed by issues and a calling that only gradually become clear, essay by essay, in the writing. There is enormous trust in this—that truth will in time come near; that God is a God of order, however mysterious and bewildering that order at times appears; that being lost is how we are found; and that we are not alone in this journey, that, as these pages attest, we are surrounded by a company of witnesses who have worked these fields and cleared these pathways before us.

For example, in the first essay, "Field," dramatizing Kriner's initial encounters with the farm's scrubbed-over acres—"crumble-down buildings full of abandoned trash; brambly former oak savanna choked with massive black walnut, ubiquitous honeysuckle, and garlic mustard; rock-laden fields, sapped as they eked out soybeans one more time"—we gradually discover that she's thinking about two fields at once: the tapped-out fifteen cultivated acres *and* the new field of thought, the spiritual vocation, the acres have called her to. "We were coming across a field full of powers and forces," she writes of those first days, "and we didn't know what to do." "So many forces hidden there," she writes, thinking of both fields, making it necessary, in Virgil's words, "to study the ways of the winds / And the changing ways of the skies, and also to know / The history of the planting in that ground, / . . . To be taught to find [one's] way."

She might also have quoted Thoreau at the beginning of *Walden*, who, after laying the foundation for the chimney of his cabin, declares, "It would be worth the while to build still more deliberately than I did, considering, for instance, what foundation a door, a window, a cellar, a garret, have in the nature of man [before] raising any [other] superstructure." It's to Kriner's great credit that she does such considering on the fly, moving seamlessly back and forth between what she learns about the clearings and fields and woods they've taken possession of and the foundational truths—sometimes dark, sometimes exultant—in her own nature, in all of ours, brought to the surface by that work. That pathways exist between the spiritual and the particular is something she knows from her other vocation as professor of literature, and each of these essays finds its way alongside of challenging, deftly quoted voices of other writers, each of whom, as she puts it in this essay about the great African American writer Charles W. Chesnutt, "looks in [her] direction" and "lead[s her] out, step-by-step, into the field he's writing from" and in doing so opens up to her the mysteries of her own heart's field.

In "Grass," framed as a "dream letter" to the American writer James Baldwin written from within the five tucked-away acres of "drought-stricken grass" the family calls the Hidden Five, the death of George Floyd forces Kriner to reckon with Baldwin's calling out white America's "innocence," its "unwillingness to know" and thus take responsibility for the continuing sin of racism. The dry grass, strikingly metamorphized by the drumbeat of Covid deaths reported in the news, a thousand a day, into a five-acre graveyard filled in less than a week, testifies to "the plague of whiteness" that she desperately tries to defend herself against. If only sin were reckoned individually, she writes, she might find herself "one of the remnant to whose account George Floyd's death would not be charged." Gradually, however, over a period of months, she acknowledges responsibility for the whole of it, "field-wide," turning away from the thought that she might have been able to pay only for her own small part and being crushed by the thought that "when I want to do good, evil is right there with me." All of this leads to one of the most striking, and foundational, turns of the book—the author "wander[ing] in the Hidden Five among the tombs" and then, dropping all pretense that she can redeem the dry grass within and without her own soul, joining with the voices of Baldwin and Toni Morrison's Pilate Dead and the beekeeper C. C. Miller who originally settled on this property in a desperate cry for "Mercy!" which is suddenly answered by Christ himself, "striding into this field, . . . crowned in oak and linden," and drawing all of their words, even this broken essay, "straight to [his] dripping fingers, to the flowers of his crown" in order to redeem them, crying out, "This grass shall live!" I find my breath taken away here, each time I read this essay.

"Forest" details an almost overwhelming attempt to return the land's dense tangle of honeysuckle and briars, grown "wild in a hundred-year isolation," to the "oak savanna with a great deal more light" it once was, lopping invasive plants and moving sheep and the impossibly tangled fencing used to confine them from one part of the woods to another, in an attempt to let "light [in] again all the way to the forest floor . . . reach[ing] the oaks that would be, the daisy-headed fleabane, the pink lantern of phlox, and the Drummond's aster who takes her time." Increasingly, it becomes clear to the writer that she herself is "a forest full of honeysuckle" and that she is lost in an inner tangle of rage and sweat and sacrifice at the impossible task. "What shall we ever do?" she asks, joining herself to the voices of George Eliot's Dorothea Brooke and T. S. Eliot's version of his wife Vivienne in *The Waste Land*, reaching toward Isaiah's vision of a world in which we "will be called oaks of righteousness, / the planting of the Lord, . . . display[ing] his glory," but finding no way there save through these overwhelming questions. And this suddenly seems to be the point—that the writing itself, clearing away not the entire forest floor but the way to a single broken-off question, is what each of us is called to; that, like Janie in Zora Neale Hurston's *Their Eyes Were Watching God*, "her arms like branches thrown up to God, asking questions," we have miraculously become, in our seemingly endless attempts to open the forest floor to light, the "four-leaf oak saplings" ap-

pearing here and there on the forest floor one fall, bits of
red reaching toward and testifying to a light and a grace
outside of ourselves and not of our own making.

"Clearing" is an account of that light coming down.
Kriner describes discovering and then, after calling the
animal rescue center, sitting in the rain with an "injured,
young great horned owl," "a giant, messed-up bird, come
down to the understory of our wrecked, wet woods,"
awaiting help. It's a kind of Annunciation, a vision of
the Lord, in his brokenness, "coming to the messed up."
Her phone dies and there is nothing to do but stare, trans-
fixed as Wordsworth was before her, by "the wonder,
the mystery, of beauty," "the bird [having] become flesh
among us." All she can do is look, seeing finally in the
owl's beauty—"His aspect was all intention—no, not intention; *attention*. Only the violet underlid occasionally
slow-closed in what [her husband] Josh called a mascara
blink (the violet did have an eyeshadow look to it) against
the gold and gray and brown"—not meaning, not an ex-
tension of human depth, not something waiting for her
to act, but the broken world itself, God having embraced
our brokenness so that we, in our failures, might be able
to simply quiet ourselves and "look back." For what else
is true beauty but "the Lord our God [coming] upon us,"
and what is true vision, what are we founded upon, but
the call to quiet ourselves and look back?

In the final essay, "Wattle" (a wooden fence, made
of stakes and interlaced branches), the inner issue that

comes alive for her has to do with the need to make order, to create a private space to think within. Haunted by Frost's "old-stone savage" neighbor's dark, self-protective claim that "Good fences make good neighbors," Kriner describes herself, having "not had a clear thought in months, let alone a clear sentence," building a wattle fence near the house so "the ducks will stay out and I can have one ordered, tidy space with some flowers, which at least looks neat." That drive—to hem in, to mask, to separate off, to consecrate—is turned one way and then another, and then, like all of the other foundational drives of this book, shattered and transformed, in small and large ways. The large way involves an attempt to move a steer onto a trailer, an act of planning and coercion and fencing and prayer that "requires perfection" and drags on for several exhausted, thirsty days only to be deeply and grandly resisted with one final, fence-clearing lunge. They've named the steer Three, and Kriner's language returns to Melville's biblical cadences as she tries to capture Three's ecstatic lunge for freedom: "how, Three breached— . . . how, he leaped like a bull off the altar, over our perfectly posted fence gate—how, he brought down whatever would compel him—how, he crash-crushed the gate as he leapt—how, he crumpled the dream of tidy order, its shifting boundary lines and false freedom, for a season—how, he felled the straight gate in his furious haste and emerged unfazed, unhurt—how, he arced into the open field, tumbling full ecstatic, sublime as a bee for his full flower." The last image echoes Emily Dickinson, and it's Dickinson's wry confession that Kriner turns to in concluding the essay and, essentially, reflecting on the volume as a whole. Successful cultivation of her own "little Circuit," Dickinson writes, would have turned her away from a larger "new Circumference" whose divine beauty and power cannot be ordered and yet, as Dickinson and Kriner both show us, graciously reveal itself to the broken, those with eyes to see even in the smallness of a child's gestures with which Kriner ends this volume, unimaginable, never fully comprehended, glory.

Thomas Gardner

Lord, have mercy

1

Field

Walking across a field we are focused on at this time now, Judd.
We are focusing on the act of walking across a field.
We will focus our attention on this gesture of walking.
We will act in the manner of moving our legs forward.
We will press our heels to the grass while we are in the process of
movement and we will extend our toes forward.
We will bend our knees as the soles of our feet press against the grass.

—Sara Wintz,
Walking Across a Field
We Are Focused on at This Time Now

*O*n a map, the shape of the land where we live is a kind of arch.

I mean, yes, it's a square. This is the Midwest; of course it's a square, with little subsquares shaded in green and brown depending on the season and whether the pasture is healthy. But a generation ago, someone sold out a thin bit in the middle. So, walking up from the driveway of Root and Sky Farm, there are almost fifteen acres of fields, then a bend through some trees toward a hidden, five-acre parcel that's inaccessible by roads, and then a descent into dense forest. There are two houses tucked into a clearing, and one of them has a wattle-fenced garden. That's where we live.

That sliver in the middle, complete with its fine pond, is treed into solitude and marked with fierce Video Surveillance and No Trespassing and No Soliciting signs—signs made persuasive by gunshot sounds that ring out from time to time. We don't go there unless the animals get out.

The outside edges of the farm are more than overgrown; there are semicollapsed barbed wire remnants along them. When Josh and I first came to look at the land, it was a mess: crumble-down buildings full of abandoned trash; brambly formerly oak savanna choked with massive black walnut, ubiquitous honeysuckle, and garlic mustard; rock-laden fields, sapped as they eked out soybeans one more time. Maybe it's a descending arch, a kind of U-shaped wallow.

It had chaos going for it, anyway, and the sort of pitch and roll that made me feel things. Just the sort of primordial parcel, I thought to myself, that one might name and order and bring into being. No idea what to do after that, of course. It felt, that first day we looked at the field, mysterious, so much, so beyond us, even with the wonder of the fuzzed ripe soybean pods between our fingers, October light across the rows and our shoulders.

In physics, a field is a region marked by forces that you can measure at each point in spacetime. There are any number of measurables: temperature, gravity, wind speed, electricity. The more we measure, the more we can define the field, its directions, its shape, and what acts on it.

People used to understand physics-type fields as a sort of soupy, spiritual matter—the aether. Aether was the pool stars swim through, luminiferous—light bearing. According to Aristotle, it was a fifth element, called by other scholars "quintessence." Alchemists sometimes sought to distill quintessence to make magic.

I'd like to distill this field, if I could.

Our own memories exerted an ethereal aura around the land when we saw it that first day. The upstate New York of my youth rolls like the sea it once was in undulant green fields edged with woods. Most of Illinois seemed ironed flat. But these fields—sandy loam with a bit of a wave—felt almost as familiar as our home country, swells of a body we'd known before.

That first day, I insisted we walk the large field along the edges of the soybean crop just turning back from green to gold. The northeast corner of the main tillable acres was a low point, and from there, the field rolled out and up to the south and rippled west, yes, like a wave, or like one of those parachutes that you riffle in gym class, everyone lending a hand. It wasn't like the Amish farms we passed in Pennsylvania—tidy flower-lined spaces in perfect order somehow. But who knew but that it might could be. Imagination's own quintessence was here; I may have been bewitched.

Yet so much entropy thickened the ethereal soup. We started our walk past a makeshift dump near the entrance to the field—a mountain of rain-wrecked couches now homes for critters, broken end tables, stained mattresses, plastic deck chairs, bags of diapers, endless empty cans of Monster energy drink. A massive trucking rig's cab and a scruffy white, lure-the-children-into-sex-slavery-with-candy van. A boat in the weeds, a pickup truck cap strewn farther out in tall grass. Out deep in the field, in the jutting finger of forest, in a big crevassing hole, another, older dump with mattresses, a coil-backed old refrigerator, random farm equipment, and a dangerous mesh pile of barbed wire and conduit. Boggled the mind how anyone got that trash out there—five acres from the house and barn—or how to get it back out, or whether you even should.

Were there forces at work on this field? Much had been done, we were sure, to the soil, to the beans. Around here, Monsanto donates to the local food pantry, big checks like the ones on *The Price Is Right* or from the Publishers Clearing House Sweepstakes, where people take pictures. If there was any order in that field, it was chemically enforced. Even words about chemicals, our own doomsday vocabulary built from books and documentaries, were a sort of entropic force over the land, cursing it. Not only big ag words either. Slow-food, organic farm-to-table consumers have their own foreclosing force phrases: "Corn and soy." "Played out, exhausted land." "Sevin." "Roundup-ready seed." "Genetically modified." "Ruined."

The language applied to the field shaped how we looked at the land and those who had lived there. Real estate agents turned us into would-be rescuers and better stewards of the place. They described the "land-baron-wannabe owner with $100,000 in back taxes," "recently displaying erratic legal behaviors," "in a legal war with the mortgage companies," with "hostile tenants."

Virgil's books and poems are fields registering forces too. This is especially true in the *Aeneid*, of course—all that war—but also in the *Georgics*. The tools of the farmer mentioned in those agricultural poems are described as "weapons the farmer / needs for sowing his seeds and raising his crops" and the field a place to "win the glory the land can offer." And what does a farmer turn over, eventually, but even more remnants of the war? They dig up "a spear, / Almost eaten away with rust," "an empty helmet," "giant bones in that graveyard." Every field is a battlefield—"War everywhere," he writes, "in the world; crimes everywhere, / In every way and every shape and form." Virgil doesn't let up: "The crooked sickles are beat into swords" and "Mars rages everywhere." Thus every field under these caesars, weathers, wars, or gods is a graveyard, force's end.

We were coming across a field full of powers and forces, and we didn't know what to do.

In 1887, Charles W. Chesnutt's story "The Goophered Grapevine" was published in the *Atlantic Monthly*, the first short story by an African American to appear in the magazine's pages. In it, a couple of northern white carpetbaggers, John and Annie, meet an older Black man, Julius, as they consider a ruined plantation they want to buy and fix up.

Uncle Julius has been working the land through slavery time and since, though the master of the plantation, Dugal McAdoo, died in the war. Julius is sitting on a log eating grapes when the couple finds him, but he willingly tells them a story as they rest. His tale relates a curse on the place—a goopher—that came into being when Mars Dugal couldn't keep the people he was enslaving from eating ripe grapes and hired a conjure woman to scare them away from the crops. Aunt Peggy goophers the vines so that a curse would fall on any field workers who eat of them, and thus Mars Dugal successfully increases his profit.

It gets worse when Mars Dugal takes advantage of the sufferings of a freedom seeker from another plantation, Henry, who has unwittingly fallen under the goopher. Henry is cursed such that his health is tied to the health of the field, waxing and waning seasonally. And each year, Mars Dugal sells Henry off the plantation after the peak of his season, making a great deal of profit because Henry is so strong. And when Henry withers in winter, Mars Dugal buys him cheaply back to his plantation, where, when spring comes, his strength will be renewed and Mars Dugal can profit from him again.

Even this doesn't satisfy the profit appetites of Mars Dugal, though, and his greed kills both the land and Henry. When a northerner comes in with a supposed miracle process to increase the productivity of the vines, Mars Dugal jumps at the opportunity. But the northerner's chemicals and his ill-advised agricultural method of digging around the roots destroys the cultivars and ruins the fields for good. Henry, who had been rooted to land in slavery, conjure-rooted, and uprooted again and again, withers like the field he's tied to. He dies and is buried next to the field he worked.

John and Annie think that the story about all the magical forces over the field is a tall tale to scare them away from buying the plantation, and they buy it anyway. But they like Uncle Julius and his stories, and they hire the older man to be their driver. And they look the other way during harvest—a worker can sneak grapes from time to time.

Chesnutt's story ended up being the first in a whole series of conjure stories in which Uncle Julius yarns on John and Annie. And they became a book, *The Conjure Woman and Other Tales*, published in 1899. Each tale contains a story Uncle Julius tells within a frame narrated by John, and each lays out something about slavery time. They instruct the northern white folks about how to farm the land, about how to deal justly and well with people in the community. They teach the carpetbaggers about slavery's curse, what it meant and continues to mean. Together, they function as something of a manual, a handbook for healing.

For the tales bring together characters—white and Black—in recovery. For vastly different and unequal reasons, they need homes, vocations, new roots. Uncle Julius and his community, barely making it after the failure of Reconstruction, are dealing with major traumas and need some sort of financial way forward; Annie is sick and in need of a new home; John needs a new field to work in and is shopping in search of one.

The stories' power comes from Chesnutt's own search for the same things his characters need. Sure, Chesnutt's peregrinations preceded the Great Migration by a couple of decades—the way he told it, his career was "postbellum, pre-Harlem." But he experienced all the experiences and felt all the feelings that made millions of race refugees leave whatever home the South had been to them. Uprooting Black people is tradition in the United States, though, as bell hooks and others have pointed out, more and more Black people are rerooting in the agricultural lands of the South, trying to heal.

Chesnutt's parents, though never enslaved, had been uprooted too. His daughter wrote, "They had had their fill of insecurity and fear. . . . Their suffrage had been taken away. Laws forbidding marriage between white and free colored people had been passed. They had now no more civil rights than slaves and were practically in the same condition." They wagon-trained from North Carolina in the 1850s, enjoying homeownership in Cleveland.

Not that the North was all that much better, though. Chesnutt's father got arrested for defying the Fugitive Slave Act when he joined a posse of Oberliners to liberate a fugitive who'd been captured. But the legal environment worked to his advantage in an abolitionist area: the warrant for the arrest misspelled Andrew Jackson Chesnutt's name, which allowed the Yankee judge to throw out the case.

Still, they were homesick. True, North Carolina was a state that would, even years in the future, remain so resistant to Black elected officials that it would raise a coup d'état to overthrow a fusionist elected government. Even so, familial roots clutched at Andrew Jackson Chesnutt—his own father was back in North Carolina. So Andrew uprooted his young family and brought them, including young Charles, who'd been born in Cleveland, back.

⌒

When I interviewed for my first professor job in my field—or, to state it more accurately, interviewed for my first professor job in what I thought might become my field if I got the job, received some mentoring, and worked hard—one of the search committee members took me to dinner. It's a standard part of the process, but an extremely awkward one. The interviewee is trying to demonstrate competency in a field the boundaries of which are delineated only as clearly as a fifty-word job announcement. She is trying to show she will surely flourish in the earth in that spot, though she has no idea whether that will be the case. The interviewer is the mighty walnut of the place, having flourished for decades, now overshadowing all the upstart undergrowth from a higher height and with a more stable root ball.

In the car on the way to the Macaroni Grill, I tried to make conversation. But I was low on ideas, having put all my best lines out for the interview with the provost and dean. Grasping, I asked what it was like to live in Illinois. This most senior professor in the English department had grown up in Iowa on a farm and, despite feeling—and regularly asserting—a certain moral advantage held by all raised in Iowa, had been keen to leave farming for literature. Illinois is mostly a farming state, which is good. But, there's always Chicago to reckon with. So he said, with a special flat, blunt abruptness to his tone that I have come to adore, "I find it a completely nondescript state."

I laughed and began, as is not uncommon with me, to babble. I told him about growing up in rural upstate New York between a strawberry farm and a dairy farm, where I picked berries with migrant workers in the cold rainy mornings of June, each leaf holding what seemed like a cup of hand-numbing water. I told him about Pennsylvania, where I went to college, with its hilly land that reminded me of the curve of a body. He must have heard some homesick longing in my voice, because he asked, "Is it your goal to get back there eventually?"

I paused for a moment, finally, and thought about what I was saying—and to whom. Hadn't I imagined that very goal any number of times? Did I want it as my goal?

"My husband and I are looking to put down roots," I said, and it wasn't a lie, exactly.

Charles W. Chesnutt was a serial transplant. He found the ancestral North Carolina his folks returned to inhospitable. The same racial prejudices as before the Civil War persisted, and a very light-skinned mixed-race child suffered even more with color-line troubles. As a young man, he wrote in his diary, "I occupy here a position similar to that of Mahomet's Coffin. I am neither fish, flesh, nor fowl—neither 'n[——],' 'white,' nor 'buckrah.' Too 'stuck-up' for the colored folks, and, of course, not recognized by the whites. . . . Now these things I imagine I would escape from, in some degree, if I lived in the North."

And of the North? He wrote, "I will go to the Metropolis or some other large city, and like Franklin, Greeley, and many others, there will I stick. I will live somehow, but live I will, and work." But he, too, was always homesick, from his earliest departures. In his first schoolteacher jobs, he wrote of a longing for home fields. In Washington, DC, looking for opportunities, he worried in his journal over "that old failing, homesickness, which I had thought myself clear of." In 1883, he left again for New York, and eventually Cleveland.

Though they differ from each other in social condition and race, the framing characters in Chesnutt's conjure stories share with Chesnutt the condition of being uprooted. John and Annie, from a Northern Great Lakes shore city, are casting about for a cure for Annie and enterprise for John. The malady from which Annie suffers is only vaguely described in the story, but her health is linked to the weather; her condition is parallel, almost ironically, to the character Henry, whose health is tied to the health of the field. Or perhaps Annie suffers from a more literal version of her author's, Chesnutt's, metaphorical homesickness. Annie's home in the North is making her sick, and she needs a new one.

Uncle Julius, formerly enslaved, was never allowed roots; he is looking to figure out his community's postbellum place near the plantation where John and Annie decide to settle. But surely his position, too, is almost as deeply affected by the waxing and waning of the grapes as his tale's Henry's: his livelihood is tied to the land. In 1866, in North Carolina, Black codes established the standards for apprenticeship that legally mandated ongoing unequal power dynamics between former enslavers and those they enslaved: "That in the binding out of apprentices of color, the former masters of such apprentices, when they shall be regarded as suitable persons by the court, shall be entitled to have such apprentices bound to them, in preference to other persons."

Granted, Julius is not an apprentice, and his former master, Dugal McAdoo, has died in the war—and further, the text indicates that he's been associated with this spot of land for his entire life. He continues to live in a cabin on the former plantation and lives off the leavings of the neglected grapevines. But no less is he in danger of vagrancy under North Carolina's 1866 codes: "if any person shall be found spending his time in dissipation, or gaming, or sauntering about without employment, or endeavoring to maintain himself or his family, by any undue or unlawful means, such person shall be deemed a vagrant, and guilty of a misdemeanor"—which offense was punishable by arrest, prison, and the workhouse. If he is untethered to the land, any hope of bodily safety depends on his getting tethered, and quickly.

For Chesnutt, northern Ohio was not especially welcoming; he learned this quite well by 1887, and even more well by the time the book version of his stories came out in 1899. He lived a couple of miles from Lake Erie's windy shores in Cleveland, and he even changed the sentences of "The Goophered Grapevine" to emphasize very recognizable Great Lakes weather patterns in the book. Annie's sickness in the story may have a source in Chesnutt's family's experience: his wife Susan had been seriously ill of the cold when they first arrived in Cleveland. His daughter's biography describes the situation: "The weather was very cold for May, and Susan could not get warm. She became seriously ill. . . . Susan and the baby did not thrive, and Charles was terribly worried."

Yet not only the need for a home but also a home field, a place in the world, is behind the stories—for the characters John and Julius, and for Chesnutt. John's need for a home manifests in a search for a new career—the vineyard for him to work. The opening of "The Goophered Grapevine" is full of John's dreams of economic prosperity in grape cultivation. He is a man searching—searching for "a locality suitable," for "what I wanted," "a place that might suit me." He thinks, "I might find what I wanted in some one of our own Southern States." That proprietary, national diction, which might rankle in a postbellum context as it headlocks the South into communion, only comes to the fore more powerfully when John suggests he might be "enough of a pioneer to start a new industry" in North Carolina, if grape culture was unknown in the region.

We might think of John as transplanting the industry with what he *thinks* is special knowhow. Prior to the war, the Ohio River Valley had been the number one wine-producing region in the country, but a crop disease had led to the abandonment of most vineyards and their reestablishment along Lake Erie. An influx of immigrants during the period only further underscored the dominance of the grape business. By the 1880s when Chesnutt was writing his goopher tale, the Lake Erie grape corridor was hitting its peak production, fueled by immigrant expertise. John declares himself to be one who "had given [grape culture] much study." The story's language, though, suggests a sort of too-academic greenness that, if we take true the conventional wisdom that it takes one to know one, I recognize.

For John as for Chesnutt, finding a new home and a new field is a deeply "radical [that is, root-level] change," and John and Annie take some time thinking about it. Yet there is evidence in the story that John is viewing the chaos of the setting of the ruined plantation as opportune. John and Annie observe the "well-nigh exhausted" soil, the vineyard's "utter neglect," the grapes "few" and "scattered"; they note the standard-to-the-genre "decayed gateposts" and the "ruined chimneys that were still standing, and the brick pillars on which the sills rested," but proclaim that they will buy it if they can be "reasonably sure of making something of it." They are full of patriotic and capitalist—and indeed, aesthetic—energy.

Chesnutt may have been long-term looking for a different sort of field to work in, a vocational field where he could put down roots too. His ambitions led him to a variety of pursuits: teaching school, stenography, languages, and education administration. But on May 29, 1880, he wrote his true longing baldly and boldly, in a manner particularly suited to a journal: "I think I must write a book." Stark as it was, though, the sentiment had been building for months, maybe years, as he'd kept abreast of contemporary fiction and its possibilities for earning a living wage.

It might suit him, he thought. Publishing had been favoring local color and dialect fiction projects. But in the fiction then ascendant, the southern Black characters functioned as relics of the old slavery times. Uncle Remus and the plantation tradition reached back into a fantasy of slavery time with elder ex-slaves telling young white women how good it was before the war, how in the good old days, the plantation was a family, Blacks and whites together, with dancing and food and laughter. Chesnutt knew he could do better than that.

Chesnutt figured he had better and longer access to the material. Even in his early twenties, he had mused in his journal, "Why could not a man who has lived among colored people all his life, who is familiar with their habits, their ruling passions, their prejudices; their whole moral and social condition; their public and private ambitions; their religious tendencies and habits—why could not a colored man who knew all this and who, besides, had possessed such opportunities of observation and conversation, with the better class of white men in the south as to understand their modes of thinking . . . why could not such a man . . . write a far better book about the South than Judge Tourgee or Mrs. Stowe?" He started collecting bits of material, folklore to weave into stories, and he started getting little bits of local color into magazines.

Chesnutt was strategic in his use of this dialect/conjure material, using it at first to get into the national magazines, and then, after abandoning it for a time, returning to it to gather material to put out his first book. And he soon realized that the stories couldn't be the sorts of "happy darky" plantation stories that most magazines wanted—even if that was a way into the magazines. His work would break the stereotype. Even more, his journal entries asserted, it would be on fire with "purpose, a high, holy purpose" that would correct and heal white racism:

The object of my writings would be not so much the elevation of the colored people as the elevation of the whites—for I consider the unjust spirit of caste which is so insidious as to pervade a whole nation, and so powerful as to subject a whole race and all connected with it to scorn and social ostracism—I consider this a barrier to the moral progress of the American people; and I would be one of the first to head a determined, organized crusade against it.

Chesnutt's crusade is a necessary exodus toward a promised land. It centers space and the creation of an integrated community. For Chesnutt, "it is the province of literature to open the way for [Black people to get recognition and equality] . . . to accustom the public mind to the idea; to lead people out, imperceptibly, unconsciously, step by step, to the desired state of feeling." The language of leading out, step-by-step, of taking position, is in the service of a dream of interracial community. Chesnutt believes in the possibility, difficult to imagine in postbellum life even when whites and Blacks inhabited the same city, of making a culture together.

Chesnutt's dream preceded King's, and Chesnutt is a pioneer—not of grape culture in North Carolina, but of that kind of peace. And young Chesnutt dreamed so resolutely—"I will trust in God and work. This work I shall undertake not for myself alone, but for my children, for the people with whom I am connected, for humanity!"

A decade after my fateful interview dinner, I had gotten the job, navigated the minefield of assistant professorship, and gotten tenure. The congratulatory letter was so kind: this offer of tenure, wrote the provost, constitutes an invitation for you to spend your entire career here. I was shocked, in a way, at the momentousness of such an offer. I wasn't so sure I had the scholarly identity or brand that my dean had hoped for in my second-year review. I wasn't sure I was cut out for having a scholarly brand at all. But I was trying to get into the field.

The book I wrote to meet the criteria for tenure is called *The Future of the Word*. And it turns out it had something to do with getting into a field, though perhaps the field was theology rather than Americanist literary studies. It is about how readers cultivate books for meaning. Alongside all creation, its argument goes, books have a future in the kingdom of God, a future in which readers participate. When we read, we amplify works, preserve them, interpret them in community, and even judge— and forgive—them. Doing so, we participate in cultivating their meaning and purpose in the love of the Trinity.

The richness of the metaphor of reading as cultivation still helps and thrills me as I read and teach. But I realize now that I hadn't thought much about *where* books might be cultivated, and whether and how it might matter if they were cultivated in one place rather than another. It's funny now, looking back, because I even mention the parable of the sower three times in the book—only to make no point about the soil or locations from which we interpret. I was reading from a real space and time, but I acted as if I were cultivating texts in some imaginary universal space—the aether, maybe.

What I did make in the book, in the acknowledgments section, was a promise to my husband. Now that the book was finished and tenure obtained, we could move on to cultivating *his* dream: a farm. He had never felt settled in a career, though he'd tried several. Ill with unrelenting and continuous migraines, dissatisfied with real estate and bond trading, he had served as primary caregiver to our children, started a small business, and then begun exploring opportunities. It would have been impossible to predict at the time of our wedding what happened when he began to read and learn about just food and agricultural production.

Maybe I should have extrapolated from that one pear tomato plant beside our apartment in Madison—he would harvest a snack on the way to the office—or the red dinnerplate dahlia called Babylon. But the move from our modest suburban house and scant half acre to a farm just as the housing bubble broke was a truly radical change in our lives, and it still feels that way.

I wanted us above all to do something good with Josh's dream to try and grow Root and Sky Farm out of a scrubbed-up parcel of sixty-some acres in rural Illinois. I wrote a soaring mission statement. We would craft "a just and sustainable community farm in northern Illinois." We would seek "to participate in the renewal and restoration of land hunted and planted by the Potawatomi and for decades cultivated by the great nineteenth-century beekeeper C. C. Miller." I was expansive, describing our hopes to grow "animals, grass, trees, and bees to improve the land in beauty and fruitfulness."

I thought we could help grow and raise delicious food that helped people eat in ways that align with their values. I thought we could build welcoming, diverse communities of neighbors, farmers, and artists. I even thought we might someday support research into better sustainable farming methods in a changing climate. Of course, it was a dubious plan, mostly because it sounded so good.

The story of "The Goophered Grapevine," or rather, the story within a story, might work as a cautionary tale for eager-beaver newcomers to the neighborhood of the plantation. In contrast to nostalgic plantation tradition stories, it described life "before the war" truthfully. The plantation meant unstinting drive toward profit for the enslavers—for the enslaved, only being unstintingly driven. Little to eat; plenty of diseases and childhood mortality; a pack of dogs after runaways; and almost enough guns and steel traps to keep them from eating the very grapes they themselves grew.

The caution of the tale for John and Annie comes partly from Julius's recounting these everyday abuses, of which any owner ought to be aware—the history of the workers they aim to hire. As if to reinforce the caution, Julius calls northern carpetbagger John "marster" when he finishes his story. It's not quite "Mars," like "Mars Dugal McAdoo" for the enslaver, but there's a chilling resemblance in the term.

I'm not sure they could hear him or his cautions, though, at least not yet in this first encounter. John's closing frame emphasizes the news coverage of his plantation, which describes it as "a striking illustration of the opportunities open to Northern capital in the development of Southern industries." There it is again, the drive for profit, profit, profit. John says the vines are thriving, though. And the workers seem to have access to the grapes—John has "a mild suspicion that our colored assistants do not suffer from want of grapes during the season"—so maybe something got through.

That first day we walked the land that would become Root and Sky Farm was one of those rare, wonderful October days, full of harvest-time glory. The field, even if conventionally sown with soybeans, was gorgeous, magic-carpeted with furry golden pods. We'd gotten permission to walk it from the real estate agent, who warned us, though, to NOT approach the house, because of the aforementioned hostile tenants. There were lots of vehicles and things by the house—but it was hard to tell if anyone was home.

But, as we got out and we were crossing between the barn and the garage toward where an abandoned old cell tower cage crowned a short rise, we heard sounds. We stopped, barely breathing, and I got past a giant trucker's cab, ducking behind a nearby van, hoping the tenants wouldn't mind us being there—or, if they *would* mind, that they might not see us to be able to confront us.

No luck, though. A woman's voice shouted, "They're behind your rig!" She had come out on the deck, a big white woman, pointing. And then a big white man—seeming, to our adrenaline-sped hearts, just as described, indeed precisely "hostile"—Can-I-Help-You-ed toward us skulkers.

Josh explained, shortly, as he was clearly also frightened, that we were told we could walk the land but not the house, and that we had permission to be there.

I was pretty much HIDING crouched behind that van during this exchange. But when the tenants turned back toward the house, in what I can only presume was some sort of pissed acquiescence to Josh's statement of rights-to-see-land, I felt some stupid emotion rise up in me, some hunger for connection and goodwill.

"But wait!" I blundered, stumbling out from behind the van, bursting with foolish do-gooder spirit. "Can we meet you?"

Now, awkward, self-deprecating friendliness has, on the whole, tended to be one of my more successful attributes. It's gotten me out of some scrapes. But this time I truly was ridiculous, the most bumbling person who's ever lived—I probably even tripped as I ran out from behind my hiding spot.

He spoke, the most terrifying "WHAT!" I've ever heard.

I'd been thinking that if we just knew each other, we could maybe work something out. Maybe they could stay in the house for a while—surely it'd take some time to figure out what we were going to do with the land. We hadn't sold our house at the time. Maybe there was some way to involve them in the project of saving the land? Maybe they could stay and wouldn't have to be evicted by the bank at the time of sale? Maybe we could all work together! Who knew?

"Can we meet you?" I repeated, reaching out with as much of a smile as I could muster.

The man's face ripped to scorn or anger or something else I couldn't name.

He flicked his hand and said, "I got nothing to do with this place."

They turned and walked back in the house, away from the field and the rig.

We never saw them again. They were evicted by the bank prior to the sale, and they left almost everything there—even that rig, temporarily—on the place.

What we found when we cleaned out the house was a mess so heinous it would take us a year to make the place habitable: cascades of used diapers, animal excrement, needles, clothes, endless DVDs, cans and bottles and kitchen garbage scattered everywhere—all evidence of unfathomable suffering. A tag was hanging on the door-knob from child welfare and social services. It chimed, "Sorry We Missed You!"

⌐

What I'm discovering here is that it seems like it might make a difference to read a book from a particular field or wood. "The Goophered Grapevine," almost everything I read, feels different here and now.

Here's an example. I used to teach Chesnutt's story as a trickster tale. We would look at the way that John, the white guy, thinks that he is so smart. He thinks he sees through Uncle Julius, and calmly proceeds according to his own course of supposedly superior knowledge. We would smirk inwardly as the narrator ends the frame with a confident speech: "I found, when I bought the vineyard, that Uncle Julius had occupied a cabin on the place for many years, and derived a respectable revenue from the product of the neglected grapevines. This, doubtless, accounted for his advice to me to not buy the vineyard, though whether it inspired the goopher story I am unable to state." How excellent he thinks he is to have uncovered the trick!

But, I would ask my students, isn't Uncle Julius the real winner? He offers the white guy what the white guy thinks he wants: an old Black man rolling his eyes and smacking his teeth quaintly over grapes, telling Uncle Remus stories. Then he proceeds according to his, Julius's, purposes. For when John buys the plantation, Julius changes from being a forage farmer to a safely employed driver. Formerly, like the poor of the land in the Old Testament, he had taken the leavings of the fallow fields during the unintended sabbath of the Civil War. At the end of the story, he's fully employed and safe from the Black codes. And he has some power in this position. In the conjure tales as a whole, we see how Julius takes Annie and John not only where they want to go, but where he wants them to go, and at the pace he'd like to take them.

Teaching the story like that had been a pleasant way to have students take something from the class, the big reveal at the end. It's always more than a little self-satisfying to share something with students that they might not have considered, making sure they get their liberal-arts-college money's worth.

Yet I'd been getting uncomfortable with the reading. For one thing, after a reading gets tied up with a neat little bow, all questions answered, it's not a live reading anymore. Meaning is no longer being made and it's closed down. Another, particularly lackluster class session led me to realize that Dr. Kriner's big reveal at the end of class—my smarter-than-thou uncovering of Chesnutt's duplicitous trickstering—sounds an awful lot like John. He's so proud of himself for figuring Uncle Julius out that he stops thinking about him as a person, stops engaging.

Uncle Julius's deep well of stories can help John, but only if John drinks from it. In the rest of Chesnutt's conjure tales, what leads him to the water? Farming troubles. When he has employee problems, crop problems, facilities problems, land problems, Uncle Julius has a story to help. They become a sort of indirect advice.

My reading of Julius as the trickier trickster requires us to believe that Chesnutt *himself* is a trickster, that, perhaps, all African American authors are required to operate in trickster roles thanks to the white frame. "We wear the mask," after all, "that grins and lies," or so Paul Laurence Dunbar, Chesnutt's contemporary, wrote.

It's not precisely improper to do so. I mean, Chesnutt's journal entry, cited above, could function like that, as evidence for the trickster's role. Chesnutt's desire to "accustom the public mind to the idea [of Black people's full participation in American culture]; to lead people out, imperceptibly, unconsciously, step by step, to the desired state of feeling" amounts to a plan to trick people into going to the right place without even realizing that they are on the way. Spoonful of sugar, and so forth.

That direction of readers' attention and opinion is maybe what all writers do, of course, but the frames that set Chesnutt up as a writer of moment, such as the ones made by William Dean Howells in the *Atlantic Monthly*, are particularly racialized. Howells links Uncle Julius's trickery specifically with the author. Howells wrote that

"the stories of *The Conjure Woman* have a wild, indigenous poetry, the creation of sincere and original imagination, which is imparted with a tender humorousness
and a very artistic reticence." See? "Sincere," but also "ret-
icent"—something of the trickster.

I think Howells is trying, I do. He wants to get
Chesnutt into the room, ally-style, and he compares
Chesnutt to Guy de Maupassant, Ivan Turgenev, Henry
James, Sarah Orne Jewett. But there's this sense of power
that he as the reviewer holds: he's like John, holding himself apart. Howells will not allow the stories to touch him
or the reader: "In some [stories]," he writes, "the com-
edy degenerates into satire, with a look in the reader's
direction which the author's friend must deplore." The
author's friend, Howells writes, should keep the writer
from this sort of thing: there ought to be no address of the
reader, no pointing finger of satire, allowed.

But at the farm, with my neighbors, I need a different relationship to Chesnutt's stories than this constant
tricking and ferreting out. I can't reject the satire or the
instruction. I need something different than a situation
in which I suggest to Chesnutt which meanings are appropriate for his trickster, which meanings will align
Chesnutt with a set of racial ideas that work for my political leanings or my whiteness. I need to let his stories
look in my direction; I need to let them come by here.

One of my students last week told me that Chesnutt
is easy. I think he means "easy on white people," which,
maybe—which, OK. But I don't feel like I get off easy if I

let Chesnutt lead me out, step-by-step, into the field he's writing from, to see what has lived—and who has died—there, and why.

Lauret Savoy, in her book *Trace: Memory, History, Race, and the American Landscape*, talks about "how exploitation of land and people are intertwined." It happens around here. We know a man whose kids go to school with ours. He works for two farms at once. One of his jobs is with a farm whose field lines are so taut and straight they seem permanently scored into the land. He works incessantly and impeccably, sheets curtaining the windows in the house they rent on the property. There's no patch for anything even remotely viney on that particular farm—so he drives three hours south each August to gather a trunk full of real watermelons. He gave us one our first year here—almost three feet long, its heart flavor-soaked. When, at his son's confirmation party, I raved over his wife's *gelatina* and asked for the recipe for *mi hijo quisquilloso*, some tone was off in our conversation. I figured it was my poor and overeager Spanish. My mentor farmer told me later what it was. "Estefania," she said to me, "I'll get the *recetta por telefono, porque su esposa* can't read."

Virgil's *Georgics* has a missional question in its first line that seems exactly what I feel when I am honest about my newcomer approach to this field. His line lays out the poem's striving purpose: namely, to find "what's right for bringing abundance to the fields." David Ferry, in his wise, wondrous translation, has written that the *Georgics* is about the struggle for "human accomplishment in the difficult circumstances of the way things are"—how to do what's good, what's right where you are.

Virgil says to start by looking at the field:

> . . . if the field's unknown and new to us,
> Before our plow breaks open the soil at all,
> It's necessary to study the ways of the winds
> And the changing ways of the skies,
> and also to know
> The history of the planting in that ground,
> What crops will prosper there and
> what will not.

It's necessary to know who will prosper in a field, and why. And what happened before. And what all the hidden forces are that bear on prosperity and harm.

It's too much. I'm relieved that that first section of the *Georgics* puts an invocation at its heart. The prayer establishes the very high stakes of the poem's mission not just for farming in general, but for Roman culture—at that time becoming the Roman Empire—just two years after the end of their civil war. The *Georgics* has always been more than a farming handbook. It is as much a way of thinking about what it means to work in the world rightly in all callings—to be good for a world that has been ravaged by war and human violence.

Maybe farming handbooks have always been about more than farming. Farming is as good as any a way to talk about being in the world. Both writer and farmer want—need—to do the right thing. So Virgil prays,

> Grant me the right to enter upon this bold
> Adventure of mine, grant that I
>   make it through,
> Pitying me along with those farmers
>   who need
> To be taught to find their way, and
>   grant that we
> May come into your presence with
>   our prayers.

⟿

That first bleared season, I woke early one Sunday morning in June. The tenants' house was still more or less a landfill. In the house in the woods where we lived, half the kitchen had just been torn off and burnt to the ground. We had no sink, even, and wouldn't for months.

But we had just set out the first pasture—no more chemicals. That morning, in bathrobe and boots, I walked through the thirty acres of woods full of gooseberry bushes and birdsong. The sun was coming up over the lip of the east's cup as I crossed the field. And yes, finally, there they were, the tiniest bits of new sprouted green pasture grass, each leaf lit like a stained glass window.

So many forces hidden there, from root to sky; and I prayed for the healing of the field.

2

Grass

You turn us back to dust
    and say, "Turn back, you mortals."
For a thousand years in your sight
    are like yesterday when it is past
    or like a watch in the night.
You sweep them away; they are like a dream,
    like grass that is renewed in the morning;
in the morning it flourishes and is renewed;
    in the evening it fades and withers.
For we are consumed by your anger;
    by your wrath we are overwhelmed.
You have set our iniquities before you,
    our secret sins in the light of your countenance.

—Psalm 90:3-8

And Conscience cried for Grace until I became wakeful.

—*Piers Plowman*

Dear James Baldwin:

Last August, on the most prominent wall space in the English department, I put up a large portrait of you. It was after the fall faculty banquet; I was still in my fanciest dress. I ripped off the professional brown paper backing of one of those office-type impressionist flower scenes. Then, with the help of a couple of colleagues who happened upon me and were taller, I set you over the central seating area. You sometimes slip a little in the frame because I am not a professional framer. In the picture, your face is surrounded by a color block of purple—you are looking up and out over everything going on in the department.

I'm writing this letter, though, not from that office, but from a field on our farm, a field we call the Hidden Five. "Often I am permitted to return to a meadow," as Robert Duncan says, and this field's just such a stage on the yearly pilgrimage of the sheep. There's no road access here—hence the hiddenness—and it's barely growing anything by way of pasture. A few flowers, mostly chicory and thistle, "whose flowers are flames lit to the Lady," as it were. My own impressionist scene:

> It is only a dream of the grass blowing
> east against the source of the sun
> in an hour before the sun's going down
>
> whose secret we see in a children's game
> of ring a round of roses told.

The hidden thing in the meadow of Duncan's poem might be the plague, or approaching ubiquitous death, that we all fall down, for any number of reasons, for any number of sins. If so, I'm pretty sure the same conditions apply here, this year.

I don't think of you as especially rural, but I can't help preferring to talk over this plague—the pandemic, yes, but also race, America—with you in the Hidden Five. I'm steeling myself for your look—up and out over this hidden field, like the glance of the Lord.

You remember that part in *Daisy Miller* where Winterbourne is talking to his aunt about Daisy?

Everything seems clear to the old bag: young, vivacious Daisy Miller has transgressed the laws of social intercourse by going to the castle with Winterbourne, and she is therefore unequivocally not a "nice girl."

Grass

"I am an old woman, but I am not too old, thank Heaven, to be shocked!" Winterbourne's aunt exclaims. "I really think," she continues, "that you had better not meddle with little American girls that are uncultivated, as you call them. You have lived too long out of the country. You will be sure to make some great mistake. You are too innocent."

Winterbourne, however, doesn't want to believe it. "I am not so innocent, aunt," he says, while he twirls his mustache.

"You are guilty, too, then!" she says.

Today, a police officer in Minneapolis, Minnesota, knelt on the neck of a Black man until well after he had died of it. The Black man's name is George Floyd. He'd just gotten over COVID-19; but he still could not breathe when the cop knelt on his neck. George Floyd was suspected of trying to buy something with a counterfeit twenty. The convenience store clerk called the cops on him, and the cop, as I say, knelt on his neck, murdering.

I don't know anything about it yet. I won't even hear about it until tomorrow. But this is a dream letter. Sons and daughters will prophesy; old men will dream dreams; young men will see visions. Middle-aged, isolated, lit-professor farmers will write crazy apocalyptic dream letters to dead authors they love.

In *Daisy Miller*, who's innocent and who's guilty of social—possibly societal—sins is at issue. When Daisy shows up at the colosseum at night with an Italian man,

Winterbourne is sure she's guilty of sexual indiscretion—"she was a young lady whom a gentleman need no longer be at pains to respect." Yet to that Italian man, Giovanelli, Daisy is "the most innocent" of young ladies. For the aunt, the question of Daisy's innocence and guilt is a matter of philosophical niceties—"a question for the metaphysicians." The aunt just wants nothing to do with her.

William Dean Howells, dean of American letters, admirer of Henry James, and the most celebrated champion of global literary realism, was with the aunt on the question of Daisy's character, though he loved the story. He believed Daisy's situation was "necessary medicine" to teach the lesson of the dangers of the "defiance of conventionalities abroad." To him, it is Daisy who is guilty, and the "medicine" of the story itself comes too late for the young girl who dies of malaria.

But Winterbourne carries Daisy's death on his conscience: he tells his aunt that "he had done her an injustice"—treating an arbitrary social distinction as a moral law. He had never understood Daisy at all outside the murderous social rules and the inevitable consequences of their breakage. But still, he lets himself off the hook: "I was booked to make a mistake. I have lived too long in foreign parts."

Daisy died for somebody's sins. Hers *maybe*, though it seems a little harsh of a punishment. Winterbourne's. Giovanelli's. Society's. America's. A mosquito's.

The pervasiveness and confusion of the responsibility for the dead rise up in me here in the grass of the Hidden Five. It feels both right and wrong to me to assign it to anyone's account or to all's.

Forgive me—I was raised at a certain time in 1980s Christendom. I begged God to come into my heart and not to send my five-year-old self to hell. This occurred just before, in fact, I was sent, if not to hell proper, then to something like it, to cancer. Surviving that cancer, I became a miracle, a sort of holy freak show, back from the realm of the dead. I didn't preach then, like you, but I gave—or bore—witness.

What we had by way of guilt and innocence was the assurance of guilt—*all have sinned and fall short*, amen? And you ask God to forgive your sin—*if we confess our sins, He is faithful and just to forgive us our sins and to cleanse us from all unrighteousness*, and it's done, gone. And you try not to sin more, but then you do, and so you ask again. Sin's power is broken, so you don't HAVE to sin—*His divine power has given us everything we need for life and godliness*—but sometimes you do. So, you build virtue, though we wouldn't have called it that—too Catholic—and sin less.

There were other kinds of sins we learned about: the sins of the fathers, generational sins, national sins. But those seemed separate from an individual's account, and far from mine. I was part of the people praying that God would turn our nation back to himself, the remnant who'd not bowed the knee to Baal. I didn't listen to secular music; I wouldn't even *think* of drinking. I wasn't even holding *hands* with boys. Surely I was innocent!

You told us yourself what that kind of "innocent" meant for Americans: guilt. I must have read a hundred times those lines about white Americans in *The Fire Next Time*, how white people don't even care to know about what they are doing to Black Americans. You laid it out: that unwillingness to know, that innocence, is the problem, is, in fact, criminal.

And there were plenty of moments when I chose innocence. In college, I recall the time Melissa and I were on the same shift in the writing center. It was a slow night, and she was doing some of the reading for her African American literature class: *Black Boy* by Richard Wright. She made some comment about how intense the book was. And I said something like, "Ugh. I don't think I could handle it—so sad! Why are you even taking that course?" It wasn't required. "I just think it's important to know about this," she said. Or something. The memory ends there.

That the scene of a single, casual conversation on a random work night with a person I've not spoken to since leaving college would be burned into my memory from 1997 to the present—I've thought of that conversation a number of times—means that I was embarrassed. I always remember the embarrassing bits more than anything else. But the plain truth is that I didn't want to be uncomfortable all semester long by paying attention to heavy, difficult suffering. I was sad enough, I thought.

Sin and responsibility always felt like ledger items to me, like those hardbound books of pale green accounting paper, the school district's hard copy of the budget, that my dad would bring home to work on.

We thought all people had their own ledgers, and the trick was to ask Jesus to get us in the black, the irony of which phrase I acknowledge. God's love for the whole world is God's ability to carry all those books home and work on them. I remember people testifying to the feeling of burdens lifted.

> He paid a debt he did not owe
> I owed a debt I could not pay
> I needed someone to wash my sins away
> And now I sing a brand-new song:
>> Amazing Grace
> 'Cause Jesus paid a debt I could not pay

But I wanted to not need the grace of canceled sin. I kept and keep calculating, hoping to find myself not as guilty: yes, I freely admit that I am guilty of 32.736 percent of the injury done in whatever case we're talking about, but the rest belongs to someone or something else. I'll ask forgiveness for only this much and will pay only for what I am responsible for.

You said in *Take This Hammer*, "Everyone on the one hand is fundamentally capable of paying his dues. But no one pays their dues willingly. . . . As long as you think there's some way to get through life without paying your dues, you're going to be bankrupt. . . . And the very question now is precisely what we've got in the bank."

That ledgering, a strict acceptance of responsibility ONLY for one's own intentions and actions, may have been behind that speech I wrote for a forensics competition way back in high school. I was pinch-hitting for another team member—original oratory wasn't my normal event. And the exact topic of the speech is lost to time. But the last line was to have been delivered in dramatic triumphant tones: "then we at last, like the Constitution, will be color-blind." Of that experience, all I remember is the dots I placed by each line as I memorized it and could say it back—and that last color-blind line. I never delivered the speech, never delivered the ultimate line: a flu epidemic canceled school and after-school activities, and I didn't think the speech was good enough to rememorize for the next competition. I was better at the interpretation category, supposedly, though that speech was my interpretation of *Brown v. Board of Education*, so.

I guess it feels different now: too trembly to think of asking Jesus to forgive me for George Floyd's death, since neither you nor time nor history will ever forgive me or white people for our innocence. I want to say that I'm not guilty, that I made up for my willful innocence by taking that African American literature class in grad school, that I never delivered the color-blind speech, even if I wrote it. I want to believe that George Floyd is not an entry in my green ledger, is not a daisy pressed into my account book, that I have a sign of forgiveness like Gabriel claimed he did in *Go Tell It on the Mountain*. But—

The mural they are going to paint weeks from now in George's memory will have his face imposed on a flower. There are flowers everywhere in front of the memorial: roses, sunflowers, and yes—daisies. Ring around the rosie. Daisies, ashes, we all fall down. Plague of color. Plague of plague too. Now we breathe it on each other, an unholy spirit. Ninety-eight thousand dead so far.

I am sitting here in the Hidden Five, these acres of drought-dried field grass thick with fleabane daisy, and I am seeing all the daisies on my ledger. Neither this field nor I am cultivated, and perhaps you would rather have nothing to do with me—I wouldn't blame you. But I am writing to you because everything I've read of you suggests two things. First, you won't let me evade responsibility or get away with lies. Second, as my spiritual director put it, "even in this life he wouldn't have told you to piss off just because you were a white woman." Which is to hope that though like many of my fellow citizens I've been infected by the plague of whiteness, you might not turn me away.

Tiffany

47

THE HIDDEN FIVE, JUNE 8, 2020

Dear James Baldwin:

It's the fire next time, this time, again. Portland and Milwaukee are ablaze—and it's not only the cities. There are road-rally-type demonstrations being organized in places like suburban Wheaton, Illinois. I heard that white people there are worrying about the church windows. Still, people lined Roosevelt Road in a honk-a-thon for racial justice. I saw my colleague in her clerical collar with her kids and their signs on Facebook. But I'm thinking less about the fires than the questions they raise. In "The Discovery of What It Means to Be an American," you talk about American writers as mostly writing works symptomatic of the tensions that exist here. These letters might well be that. But you said "the time has come, God knows, for us to examine ourselves, but we can only do this if we are willing to free ourselves of the myth of America and try to find out what is really happening here," and I'm trying.

Here, in rural Illinois, it's pandemic quiet and dead-summer hot in the streets. But white folks on the Town Forum Facebook page are sure that demonstrators are coming, that they are all looters and thugs—outsiders. They are sure these people are being bussed into local communities by communist organizations. Forum posts mention the Second Amendment often, the make and model of firearms oftener. And demonstrations have arisen in nearby towns—Crystal Lake, Woodstock—there's even one in Huntley. They flash dubiously across the page: the Belvidere Walmart at 4 p.m. Residents of this town were so upset that a network of alerts was established in a Neighborhood Watch social media space so they could be ready and girded with the Second Amendment if things were to go down here.

The cruelty of the Town Forum Facebook page is breathtaking. I'd leave the group, but it seems like our farming selves need those five thousand members, especially their neighborhood-watching eyes in case our animals get out. It's happened on more than one occasion that animals have wandered through the neighborhood yards. Our sheep, Liver, got all the way to Indian Oaks Park before someone called the police to help him home. Our pigs dug up some neighbors' lawns and we had to sow liberally both grass seed and free, silvopastured bacon. A couple of cows liked the next pasture over a little better and decided to visit. The Forum was useful in such situations: members would post a picture of our escapees, and we could go get them. But these days, it makes us ill to pay attention to the Forum—we fume over various posts at dinner, upset the children. We haven't been seeing any real people because of the pandemic, only these incredibly mean, racist words.

Don't get political, the rules of the Forum state: no race-baiting. But the only thing the admin of the Town

Forum deems "politics" is the other side's opinion. "Race-baiting" seems to be defined as even mentioning racism as existing. On the one hand, it is clear that it is all talk and no one means anything by it, but it is as clear on the other hand that they *do* mean it, because virtual meaning, virtual meanness, is all anyone has.

I'd been home, home, home with sheep, moving them through the pastures toward the woods, trying to write in between, which mostly meant a lot of checking death statistics from the pandemic and demonstration statistics about the aftermath of George Floyd's death. They got to me, racking up like that, and the Town Forum Facebook page got to me, and then I'd had enough.

I tried to get the administrator of the page to have lunch with me—I'd buy, I said, and we could eat in a public place, in a park, with masks or whatever. That last bit was a mistake, mentioning masks. And yes, I called her out publicly to invite her—the page had been so mean that I was fed up. But I do want to meet her, even if my invitation was drawing attention to the all-talk-ishness of her bravado. I am longing to know who she is and *why* she fosters such a forum. *Don't do it*, someone commented to her—*or if you do, bring gun and backup*. People defend her, who know her in real life, how she's done so much for them, best friend in the world, etc. She posts these worshipful pictures of her daughter too, that, as a proud mother myself, I really understand. She wrote me back that she would let me know when she had availability.

Demonstrations are sort of the thing everyone is doing right now, so one has to suspect one's own intentions. (My dear James Baldwin, I am not so innocent.) I decided I wouldn't travel to demonstrations in Wheaton, where my colleagues are, or other towns slightly closer, where I don't know anyone. Going to those places might come from a desire to be seen as good by people—and besides would mean shirking farm duties. But not going at all seemed out of the question: I'd be guilty of silence, the gentrified country squire taking the air in the field.

So—and I was improvising here—I made myself a sign: "THE LORD LOVES JUSTICE Psalm 37:28" on one side and "Let's Pray and Work for Racial Justice" on the other. I painted it with leftover paints from when the kids were little; Fiona helped me. I had to look things up—did I need a permit to march if I brought the kids? It seemed unclear from the town code, and you could just never tell what would happen, so I decided to leave them home.

While the sign was drying in front of the fan, I got all dressed up in a pretty, navy blue polka dot dress and a straw cowboy hat; with my red hair, I was red, white, and blue—still American, even if I critique. I put a picture on Facebook of the sign, not me, and crafted a message asserting the right to demonstrate in the face of injustice. And I did a solo walk around town, just me and my sign, just a prayer walk by some innocent young American, trembling with fear and mocking herself for playing all her little-white-girl-in-a-farmer-hat games.

I walked down the hill into town, praying, stopping to talk to a few stoned-sounding guys in a hot rod, receiving some honks and waves, nervously laughing off a smart remark by the bar with outdoor picnic tables. It was so stupid. What was I even doing? Like I was going to stop some rolling tide of injustice right there with my little homemade sign. I had more or less walked off the farm, skipped whatever making-dinner-type-thing I was going to do just then. I had moved the sheep first, before I went, but still. Did I even feel better after? Was feeling better what I was after?

I wanted to be on the right side, doing the right thing, I guess, like an action would be evidence that I wasn't guilty—a signal that I was one of the remnant to whose account George Floyd's death would not be charged. I knew enough to feel bad about this line of thinking—mostly because it was all about me, and so I tried to refocus during the walk, to pray as hard as I could for George Floyd's family. I imagined what it would be like to lose him as a father, as a son. I thought of what it would have been like to have been him. My own fear while walking alone in a Second Amendment-centered town I tried to redirect toward a consideration of the suffering of those walking while Black—like Garnette Cadogan told us about.

That was Wednesday. The megachurch we attend decided to have a new, drive-in parking lot option as a way to hold pandemic church this Sunday: Park and Play, they called it. Yes, the country was on fire; yes, one hundred thousand people in the US were dead from COVID; yes, the president was photo-opping with an upside-down Bible in front of a church to assert his moral superiority over the demonstrators he was tear-gassing; yes, George Floyd was murdered, and Breonna Taylor, and Ahmaud Arbery. But we would drive to this new, rich, clean, mostly white church with acres of property separating it from any street, and park, and play.

We would not be holding up names of the dead, nor proclaiming freedom to the captive, nor demanding, "HOW LONG, O LORD?!" We were part of the welcome team; we would hold up cheerful welcome signs as cars came in. I got up early to paint the signs on Sunday morning—agonizing. And scheming: could I communicate the sort of message I thought was better than "Welcome Back!" if we made our own signs rather than using the signs provided? Could I acknowledge what was happening? Assert a theological response? In three-word-max signs?

A wicked and adulterous generation asks for a sign. I had three signs, one for me and one each for the kids. I did one "Welcome!" because I've been a goody two-shoes for a long time and usually at least pretend to follow the rules. I did one "Things Are Dire." because they are dire—disease, lockdown, lynch law—and I needed to say it. And then I turned to Julian of Norwich for the third, because I needed something encouraging, but not a lie, something ultimate. It said, "all shall be well." Four words, but they were short.

All of my signs were coded messages, and I was even worried enough to decapitalize the "A" in "all" so that "all shall be well" would not assert ALL like "ALL LIVES MAT-TER." Julian's words are backed by the credibility of plague and anchoritism, by six hundred years of amens. But it wasn't good enough for me, suddenly. By the time I was filling in the letters with bright aqua paint, I was crying. Stroke by stroke, I couldn't stop crying. I felt like I was in the middle of Julian's vision, except instead of the flowing and flowing and overflowing of Jesus's blood for her and all of us, it was that unstoppable flow of white woman tears.

I kept painting, but also kept crying. I called a friend who's married to the pastor to talk me down, because it was getting time to leave and I was still crying. I could barely speak to explain the situation. There was no way to be justified here; there was no way for me to be right. He was dead, George Floyd—and so many were dead, and I was part of a church painting selectively applicable wel-come signs. There is no way to arrange the numbers in the ledger that makes up for the fact that debts have been incurred and dues are owed.

At the church, I tried to pull myself together as the welcome team huddled up—my mask covered most of my distress. As we were gathering and laying out instructions for the day, the pastor called me. This was nice of him—it's a large church, and he was trying to be kind, to see if I was OK after hearing about me from my friend, his wife.

I couldn't receive it that way, though. "Don't worry," I told him, "I won't make a scene." That was mean of me, especially to a guy who has actually and faithfully prayed for my livestock when I've texted him in a panic that the pigs were out and missing. He just takes it whenever I speak cruelly about the church he represents, which has happened more than once—more entries in the ledger.

Eric, one of the few African American members of the church, is the head of our welcome team. We share little bits of things about ourselves when we get together. His son's an actor; his garage door has had problems for years since a storm; he'd been moving in and out of some roles at his company, trying some new things. Sunday morning, Eric shared about his responses to George Floyd's murder and asked for support from the church for African Americans. It had been quite a wake-up call for him. He'd been operating in white worlds his whole life, he said. But he'd realized this week that George Floyd for him was like Rodney King for his father.

Everyone loves Eric as much as one can in the cordial-but-not-close relationships that seem to be fostered by the welcome team as I've experienced it. I'd wanted to be on *his* team as soon as I met him—everyone did. So team members wanted immediately to be as supportive as they could be. I heard one woman, who always volunteers with her husband, say, "We've *never* thought of you as Black!"

In our town the Black people—all 0.54 percent of them, by the 2010 census, though the demographics have changed some—get thought of as Black. We got a phone call one time from a woman who lived in our house in the 1940s and '50s, after it had been an inn. She told us it didn't just *look* like a sundown town here; it *was* one. There was a Black window washer she knew, who'd help with the house, and a bell that rang at six o'clock, a warning to Black workers.

It hasn't gotten much better these days. Terry and Kendra live in town here—he's Black, she's Mexican. People finger the N-word into the dust on their car's rear window. Old high school frenemies of Kendra's—she grew up in town here—send Terry letters saying their children aren't his. People skulk around their yard. He coaches Little League, arranges open gyms to get the boys moving in basketball, watches kids' sports games for the joy of it—a joy unspeakable and full, it seems to me, of glory. Kendra has told me she just hopes that their kids' teachers here in town are young, at least a little educated. They raise their boys responsible, athletic—top grades and all that—but they're no fools.

I found out this weekend that a young white woman from town had seen my pathetic walk. She decided to organize a bigger walk—a march for our small town—and there was a new Facebook group, Citizens for Equality, and she invited me and the kids to join them. It was this evening. Maybe twenty people came—Terry and Kendra called in Kendra's relations to help support them, and they filled out about half the mini-crowd. Terry had a giant Black Lives Matter flag and Kendra held a sign in one hand, "MY BLACK SONS MATTER." There were a fair number of young white people who brought extra recycled cardboard signs. We walked down an inner street parallel to Route 20—people watching from porches, people driving by. We turned on Main Street past an insurance agency that had put a giant B, L, and M in the windows and stopped to take pictures there. Then we turned off the main street toward the park. We passed one yard full of retired military vehicles, including something tankish; as we got close, they began to rev, and we fell silent.

At the park, where we ended, we knelt for nine minutes in the pavilion, and I prayed.

It did not feel like paying dues, nor especially like doing anything. I came home to the field and the sheep.

Tiffany

THE HIDDEN FIVE, AUGUST 3, 2020

Dear James Baldwin:

So, in *Just Above My Head*, Hall says that "everything a white man says to a black man is a confession, though the white man never knows it. Sometimes I sing because I'm happy, true, and sometimes I sing because I'm free: but sometimes I sing because it is so grinding down to spend one's life listening to confessions."

Fine. Maybe I won't grind you down anymore—I've been calling you up here, in a manner, but don't hear much down the line. I have a sense, as they say, that you'd just tell me to read your books. Fine. I'm doing that. But there are other ways to consider this land, these acres, than yours. This morning in the Hidden Five, I felt Walt Whitman coming into the field, hot for a reckoning.

He has so many good lines. I feel often, reading him, the same thrill of expanse and abundance that I feel when I read about the kingdom of God in Scripture, leaven in the dough. I feel the lines of "Song of Myself" rising up in me, the rhythm moving me forward.

> Swiftly arose and spread around me the
> peace and knowledge that pass all
> the argument of the earth,
> And I know that the hand of God is the
> promise of my own,
> And I know that the spirit of God is the
> brother of my own,
> And that all the men ever born are also my
> brothers, and the women my sisters
> and lovers,
> And that a kelson of the creation is love,

And limitless are leaves stiff or drooping in
       the fields,
And brown ants in the little wells beneath
       them,
And mossy scabs of the worm fence,
         heap'd stones, elder, mullein and
         poke-weed.

He, Walt Whitman, must know the Hidden Five and its stiff and drought-drooping leaves! And here he is striding across the field to me in my sinnerman misery right here. Work shirt, middle aged, beard not yet irretrievably icky. And he calls out, resonant and mighty, "Undrape! you are not guilty to me, nor stale nor discarded—"

He declares me and himself innocent in an Eden of his own making—a thousand-acre green. It's an edgy declaration, but Whitman does not back away. In section 8, he swats flies away from the baby in the cradle, refusing original sin and the domain of the Lord of the flies. He traces the life span as baby turns presumably to fornicating youngster and then to suicide. He enters into the den of urban vice, the very place itself not outside his consideration. There is no narrow gate that few find; rather, "The big doors of the country barn stand open and ready." Come on in.

The idea that Whitman doesn't believe in my sin isn't something I'm meaning merely to rag on, or I wouldn't bring it up. Since I'm white-people confessing here,

I frankly confess that I have cried reading the line "Undrape! you are not guilty to me" and would be in grave danger of lifting the hem of my own garment if Whitman asked me to, right here in this field.

But so many of the lines would appeal to you too! For who believes in creation's love keel more than you? You just as edgily as Whitman open your books with sexy bits, asserting the body, daring people to be too innocent to handle your work.

Today, with Whitman in the field, I was reading Ask Polly, a column by Heather Havrilesky, from *The Cut*. I forget how it came through my feed on my phone. I'm hellishly distractible these days. But the title was "I feel ashamed of almost everything," so of course I clicked despite being decidedly not their "women with stylish minds" target audience. The supplicant used a pseudonym, "Desiccated," which struck me as appropriate for the Hidden Five at this point in the summer. Dessicated's shame wasn't precisely about complicity in systems of racial oppression, about having George Floyd and millions more on one's conscience. But all of her shame was shame I have too—other sorts of entries in the ledger—very American. If we were pouring out confessions and such, I had plenty along her line.

Polly wrote back to Desiccated that people need to simply stop being ashamed of their existence.

"Shame prevents you from treating yourself like a person who deserves things," she writes. In Polly's shame-free dream life, one takes up space, slows others down: "I like to tax the patience of others. I like to truly assert myself, my needs, my musing thoughts, my fucking physical presence. Lately I've been through a few gigantic challenges, and I'm more of a pain in the ass than ever, and it just feels *right*."

There is another way, she says: "In a void of shame, you see people thriving and looking hot and being smarter and cooler and younger and cuter than you, and you just feel happy, the happy you might feel when gazing at a giant strawberry pie first thing in the morning and saying GOOD FOR YOU, PIE, and then saying CAN I EAT YOU, BUDDY?"

I thought while reading, dang, Walt must be loving this. Polly could be writing "Song of Myself" as an advice column: "I want you to feel my love and my shameless-ness knock you over like a big-ass wave and then grind you into the sand." Is that a rephrase of the moment when Whitman's narrator of the poem gets dashed with "amorous wet" and becomes one with the sea? If "Song of Myself" doesn't turn you over and grind you into the sand, I'm not sure anything will.

"You don't attach a fucking MORAL to everything," says Polly.

"What blurt is this about virtue and about vice?" says Walt.

"RIGHT?!" they say together, mouths full of pie, and it is a pie picnic in the dry Hidden Five.

Light as such a thing might sound in the face of national racial reckoning and the plague, you, James Baldwin, might not be as far from this as it might seem. If only the narrator of *Giovanni's Room* had been able to resist the shame! Maybe Giovanni would still be alive and they would all be at the welcome table together.

I just got back from visiting family out east. Josh hadn't wanted me to go or to take the kids. Whenever I go away, he gets unsettled, and sweetly mourns, "You're leaving me!" Not so sweetly this time did he point out the plain truth that going during a pandemic was morally problematic. Sure, we'd seemed to escape the pandemic since whatever flu it was he'd had back in March. But even driving across the country feeling well, we might have the disease already. Yes, no one had died in the county I was going to, and yes, few people there seemed even to believe the disease is anything more than some kind of conspiracy designed to bring down the nation. But facts were facts: people's lives were on the line, and I might infect them.

But, if there wasn't much pandemic there, it would be just the cross-country travel risk. We could stay quarantined until we left for my parents' house, bring our own food, wear masks, only pee and get gas on the way, right? I wanted to see family. We hadn't seen anyone for months. We didn't go anywhere. I had done seven years of work without a break—including a summer study abroad program that had taken two years of overtime to plan. I had an essay overdue to an editor who was kindly sending reminders; my book wasn't getting written because I was just doing farmwork whenever a crisis arose—often—and I was not feeling very appreciated for doing work I felt was not my job. We never, ever go on vacation. And this was supposed to be my sabbatical! Surely I deserved a small break—just a few days with my mom and dad and siblings! I wasn't going to a stadium for a political rally, wasn't popping over to Paris for the weekend. The kids' doctors gave hearty approval too: things would surely get bad this coming fall, they said, so travel while you can.

And the North Country is utterly wonderful in summer. My parents' house isn't a bit like a farm—there's no dirt anywhere, and the dishes are always done. I could sleep comfortably even on the area rug in the living room because there's some sort of springy padding underneath it, but I don't; I walk on its pillowy splendor, because Tiffany's room—they call it Tiffany's room—has got a special mattress topper that makes it even better than the rug. And outside, there's a screened-in porch, and the lawn is just so, all bird feeders and apple trees that actually grow apples. Their garden doesn't have weeds, and grass doesn't overtake the raised garden beds because they trim them all the time with a fancy string trimmer. My son plays basketball on the paved driveway. Which is to say that they have a paved driveway that they get reblacked every year by a young man who has made good after some rough times. And we go out for dinner at Sackets Harbor, just Mom and my sisters and me, and they drink wine and I eat expensive ice cream lakeside.

The kids and I went on a Sunday. Hardly a bit of traffic, and the whole trip was marvelous. It was like the pandemic barely existed. There were mandated masks at the store and church, but they had Little League games and outdoor church with *singing* in a tent and outdoor fitness classes in the parking lot where we got one parking space each. I wrote all day long on my birthday and handed in that overdue essay just before my birthday dinner—and the editor responded with a marvelous compliment right away, which never happens. My birthday dinner included veggies from the garden on the grill—cooked on a mat that keeps the grill from getting dirty, yet also doesn't melt, by some sort of weird magic. Living the dream.

The Dream, Ta-Nehisi Coates says in *Between the World and Me*, is "perfect houses with nice lawns. It is Memorial Day cookouts, block associations, and driveways. The Dream is treehouses and the Cub Scouts. The Dream smells like peppermint but tastes like strawberry shortcake."

Grass

I don't mean to suggest Whitman eats much pie. He certainly advised against it in "Manly Health and Training, with Off-Hand Hints toward Their Conditions," republished in full in 2016 in the *Walt Whitman Quarterly*:

> In our view, if nine-tenths of all the various culinary preparations and combinations, vegetables, pastry, soups, stews, sweets, baked dishes, salads, things fried in grease, and all the vast array of confections, creams, pies, jellies, &c., were utterly swept aside from the habitual eating of the people, and a simple meat diet substituted in their place—we will be candid about it, and say in plain words, an almost exclusive meat diet—the result would be greatly, very greatly, in favor of that noble-bodied, pure-blooded, and superior race we have had a leaning toward, in these articles of ours.

But meat isn't exactly value-neutral, and since I'm judging here anyway, it seems to me like low-carb diets are just another shade of the Dream. Some nights, we work on the farm until after 9 p.m., moving each individual meat chicken—some two hundred—into roofed and netted enclosures for the night so that the neighborhood owl, lately making himself known, does not gut them. The chickens sometimes screech and slap with their wings when picked up. That's a lot of work for a diet full of meat, to say nothing of the chilling sound of what Whitman's after, that noble-bodied, pure-blooded, superior race.

Back at the farm while we were gone, Josh wasn't feeling well. He's chronically ill with headaches, and constantly exhausted because of farmwork, but he'd been even more exhausted than usual these days, even early in the day. It was probably nothing. We'd been sure he'd had COVID with that flu in March—scary difficulty breathing, etc.—but there had been no tests to be had anywhere those days, and no doctor would see him, just in case he *did* have it.

But tests were making their way into the boondocks now, and he was a farmer's market worker with a moral obligation to protect the people whose food he provided, so he'd decided to get a test. On Friday, after my birthday week of bliss, Josh called with the news that (1) he had tested positive for COVID, and (2) they calculated that he had caught it at the farmer's market the day before we left to go to New York. Which meant that the virus was making its way into Josh's body during the last eighteen hours BEFORE the kids and I left our Illinois town. Which meant we might have been exposed.

We didn't/don't know how/when the disease makes its way through a body and begins to colonize other bodies. It was, however, perfectly, lucidly clear that it MIGHT have hitched a ride into Jefferson Country with us. It MIGHT, right at that moment of learning the news, very well be making its way into my saintly and asthmatic and autoimmune-disease-ridden mother, who had hugged us without reserve throughout the week. Or, gosh, into my precocious niece Charlotte, who'd had some intense breathing troubles early in childhood, who'd been offering me tidbits of writing advice on my birthday.

I, Americanly, had chosen to buy in to the strawberry shortcake pie dream over helping my husband on the farm and protecting my family. And now, dues were coming due.

I had a come-to-Jesus with Walt Whitman recently—lines from his early 1850s notebooks felt wrong in a way I'd never taken fully into account.

> I go with the slaves of the earth equally with
>   the masters
> And I will stand between the masters and
>   the slaves,
> Entering into both so that both will under-
>   stand me alike.

The lines' proclamation of equality, so celebrated as a democratic vision, suddenly seemed to me bitter, as if I'd never noticed how willing Whitman was to go with the masters. And the problem is that declared equality between "masters" and "slaves" would be a misnomer, since if the dichotomy between them collapsed, there would be no enslaved persons—and especially no masters. There is no liminal standing-between on this particular question. There is guilt; there is responsibility. A person can't go with the masters if they go with the slaves. To make a slave equal to the master is to shatter mastery and slavery all together, and all that's left are the broken pieces; "we work in fragments," says Willie James Jennings.

The problem with feeding ourselves on all the meat and all the pie, on proclaiming the expansiveness of our own individual souls, is that if we don't prefer others' needs to our own, we tend toward enslaving them to our own.

⟿

At the beginning of *Giovanni's Room*, when you use Whitman's line "I am the man; I was there," I think you are using the line far more biblically than Whitman was. I think you were thinking of Nathan and David from the Bible: YOU ARE THE MAN! who stole the beloved sheep of the poor man. Whitman doesn't mean it that way, but I think you do. The narrator of that book—also named David—had Giovanni on his conscience as much as Winterbourne had Daisy.

Whitman seems like he doesn't have much use for this sort of conscience. He dropped the slaves/masters line, though. The lines got reworked in the book—as so much of the book has been reworked, and its supposed collapsing of racial dichotomies was replaced, in section 21 of the poem, with a vision of female and male equality, of the union of body and soul. How can you not believe in sin when you've seen humans on auction?

And, for all the importance of the culture and space for abundance that helps a person toward real love, I think even Ask Polly's Polly believes in sin too. For she caveats often: "Because when you're SHAMELESS, you take up space whenever you feel like it (mostly when you're alone, not in a rude way!)" or "Out in the world, I am so considerate, mind you!"

⟜

My mom didn't get sick. Charlotte didn't get sick. It's now been almost enough time to suspect that we've escaped it entirely. But I know I am just as guilty as if they'd become an uptick on the death tally. *If you even look at a woman lustfully,* so forth. Somebody always pays—and it's usually somebody else, usually the least of these. David begged God for the life of Bathsheba's child, but he died, poor lamb, poor daisy.

Josh is still horribly sick, even if he's been deemed noncontagious and recovered by a doctor who's still not seen him. He can't breathe well; he can't do much at all—bare minimum on chores. The farm is looking even rougher than its usually rough state. Now that we are home, I substituted for Josh this weekend at the farmer's market, since we'd had negative COVID tests. But he was too sick, doing chores while I was at his market, to notice that one of the lambs, Julian, didn't come in with the rest of the flock to the water.

I had a sense, as they say among my Pentecostal people, on Saturday night when I was out for evening chores, and so I went looking. I found Julian way out in the field at the edge of the jutting finger of forest, tangled in a fence, one hoof twisted around and around in electric fence wire. In a panic, I called for Josh to bring scissors, and held and crooned the tangled lamb. Josh was so sick that after walking the distance with the shears from the truck to the bit of woods where we were, he lay on his back on the ground in the field, breathing with difficulty, while I unwound my beautiful, theological lamb. I fed him plantain and burdock leaves and sat with him until night came. Julian lived. But he lost that hoof the next day—it just fell off.

Julian, my dear daisy, hopping along behind his fellows. How shall all be well? I am responsible for you too.

It came through on the news last week that the police officer who shot Michael Brown in 2014 will not be charged.

There is not enough evidence, the prosecutor said: "Can we prove beyond a reasonable doubt that a crime occurred? The answer to that is no."

Well, but there is always Michael Brown's dead body for evidence, I suppose, his yellow socks a glinting goldfinch as his pant leg lifted up at the cuff, there on the hot, hot road.

Sometimes in this field, so alone, I hear voices, dream dreams. Song sparrows? My mom says it's Satan accusing me. I have no doubt of this. But as my spiritual director Rhonda says, often Satan's accusations are just true things said mean.

Tiffany

THE HIDDEN FIVE, AUGUST 15, 2020

Dear James Baldwin:

It is blazing, beat-down, horrible-hell hot in the Hidden Five. The sky is magical, vault-of-the-heavens type thing; the full dimensions of the clouds are finally perceptible.

Yes, sometimes the Hidden Five is beautiful as a certain sort of field is beautiful—undulating, bending toward and away, longing as things that exist long. I climbed up a hunting stand last November to take a look—the charcoal-bare tree boundary and the brown and tan scrub across the sweep of vision, with thin candles of green between. And there was this pale, miracle sort of light in the sky that felt rare, like it just might all be made new some-time. Maybe the kingdom of heaven *was* at hand. I took a photograph. The panoramic lens bellied the field out toward me—either coming home to me, or possibly, emerging in and from me too. The bending of the image like a groan yearning for the new creation.

That is not the vibe now, though. Now, it's all Cana-dian horseweed and some other kind of early-to-seed grass I don't think we planted—and thistles. The mixture of grazing grass and hearty legumes we spent all our money on didn't seem to find good soil—I'm tempted to make some sort of joke about Onan, all this seed spilled on the ground by those jokers who planted it, but I don't even know them.

I remember when I gave one guest a tour just in the hot spell after they had disced it; I had to fake optimism. The dirt was as orange as presidential pancake makeup, the furrows baked to terracotta. And now these last weeks, it has blazed with heat and wind, though something has grown since then—tares. Lo, an enemy hath done this, I'd like to say, but it feels inevitably our own fault. This is the ground where we dig our good intentions, or would, if we could break up the soil.

I'm here in the Hidden Five now because we had to separate the sheep: should have done it sooner, of course, if we'd hoped to seriously delay the breeding. We left the rams in the woven wire fence fields across the farm, half-crazy with lust; and I have taken charge of the ewes, daily wending through the scrub with its sandy-tan, caterpillar-like stem tops, to see if there's anything they'll eat. I move the fences strand by strand, square by square. Smeared with sheep hair, sweating under the endless swelter, I stomp down fierce weeds along the netting, walking it down. Thirteen hammer strikes per fence post to penetrate the drought-packed dirt, grasshoppers snicking a sort of helicopter whirr when I walk. I drag an orange snow sled laden through the would-be alfalfa and grass with a fifty-pound salt block, marine battery, grounding rod, sledgehammer, and buckets of water. It is so, so hot.

Josh has been sick for weeks now with whatever comes after a COVID that hasn't left—a languishing misery. I am taking on as many chores as I can, but not graciously, despite believing in the virtue of helpfulness. I'm evilly cranky, ungenerous, wanting to be worshiped for the great sacrifice of my sabbatical hours. I'm not writing much, except about my sins for the Ignatian exercises, and I lost the pen out of my pocket somewhere on the way out here today. If that's not a sign, I don't know what is. The pen in question was only a six-dollar fountain pen from the craft store, and there was already a crack in the plastic barrel, but we live a half hour away from the store. I comforted myself dourly that at least it was unreliable in ink delivery. I'd been having to keep licking the nib or dipping it in the coffee thermos—I can't even be properly pretentious.

The death toll is spiking again, a thousand people a day, and I just keep checking it. The other day, darkly, I thought, what if the Hidden Five was a graveyard? That day, instead of writing in what little time I *did* have, I looked up municipal planning standards for burial grounds. Then I calculated how many American graves would fit here, laid out in rows, militarily almost. Do you know, the Hidden Five would be full in less than a week? All those dead bodies, a field full of folk.

⁀

Piers Plowman was only a matter of a class period or a class and a half in my medieval/Renaissance course in college. But I remember, even twenty years later, the thrill of the alliterative lines, the way they percuss into the body. And this one terrifying passage, which I wrote down in a commonplace book:

> For Jesus like a giant with an engine comes
> yonder
> To break and beat down all that may be
> against him,

> And to have out of hell every one he pleases.
> And I, Book, will be burnt unless Jesus rises
> to life
> In all the mights of a man and brings his
> mother joy
> And comforts all his kin, and takes their
> cares away. (XVIII.252-57)

That's no sissy Jesus, I'd like to tell Zora Neale Hurston, who scorned such things. And the future of the written word itself is tied to the God-man's resurrection, to the comfort of the brokenhearted? Yes!

I'm reading *Piers Plowman* now, alongside your books. I feel such a closeness to the narrator, Will, who dresses himself up like a shepherd, or maybe like a sheep, and goes into the field. He's a wandering sinner mess, "in habite as an heremite unholy of works." I guess he's as corrupt as all the clergy he's going to rail at through the next twenty passus. They are hypocrites, and so, it seems, is he, prone to wander, as it were, not writing much—or certainly not settling any of it into final drafts, anyway. Who knows what to do, in the end, with a vision? Julian reworked hers for decades.

In *Piers Plowman*, Will is longing to learn the way to the castle of Truth, the way to live in the Truth. The poet says, "When all treasure is tried, Truth is the best." And maybe that's what I want more than anything—to be for real, for true, not so longing for fame or reward, not so much requiring to be adored—to just acknowledge the whole of it, the sin of it. The edition I opened up says on the first page, "*Piers Plowman* is a poem with the power to change your life."

I know you know all about this too, with all your characters' lookings into mirrors, John Grimes, Leo Proudhammer. But people panic at the mirror, or think maybe we don't have to look, if we just keep working, keep moving, keep insisting on our accomplishments, or our rights.

The poem *Piers Plowman* brings this problem to life in the character of Lady Meed, who represents the idea of deserts, rewards, rights, and profits. Meed is the reward we think we can earn, the reward we think we deserve, that thing we think surely we can pay for, buying our way out.

To *marry* Meed in the poem is to link one's life to her system—*I'll just take my rights and get what I deserve and pay for my mistakes, if I make any*. It seems, if anything, American to think like this, though of course *Piers Plowman* came to be in a court system of reward and favor and payback. *I deserve this or I just(ly) want that because I did this thing for the king.* Which might not be so far from American political life either, come to think.

But who can pay off the sins that have been committed? Trying to assert that we aren't guilty because look, we are infinite, we are the poet of the body and the soul, or because see here, we deserve things, or because surely we are on the right side, or even because come on, we have earned our way and sacrificed so much—these don't work at all. For who can ever pay enough?

The other day, when I was complaining about the farmwork I was doing while he's sick, Josh said, "I don't want you to help me. When I think about how much I will owe . . ." Of course, he can't do without the help, because the farm is far too much. Meed will never work. He has nightmares about me leaving him, poor dear.

By making achievement personal, a life based in Meed makes sin seem individual too, something you could name as if the whole person were that sin: Wrath, Glutton, False, and other allegories. But *Piers Plowman*, set on that whole "field of folk" canvas, shows how sin works beyond the individual, field-wide too. That the field doesn't get fully cultivated in the poem as it should, that it doesn't bear fruit, is something that doesn't just result from an individual's failing. Sin moves from real persons to social orders to cosmic forces in a frightening, subtle slippage. In this way, the working of sin from sinning, as Rudolf Bultmann would have it, operates along multiple trajectories, entrapping the sinner beyond their individual, meedy deserts.

Piers Plowman shows us how sin manifests on a physical level too, in the body itself. Envy, for example, "was pale as a sheep's pelt, appeared to have the palsy." And,

> Like a leek that had lain long in the sun
> So he looked with lean cheeks, louring
> foully.

> His body was so blown up for anger that he
> > bit his lips
> And shook his fist fiercely, he wanted to
> > avenge himself
> With acts or with words when he saw his
> > chance.
> Every syllable he spat out was of a serpent's
> > tongue;
> From chiding and bringing charges was his
> > chief livelihood,
> With backbiting and bitter scorn and bearing
> > false witness. (V.81–88)

It's Psalm 32, right?

> While I kept silent, my body wasted away
> > through my groaning all day long.
> For day and night your hand was heavy
> > upon me;
> > my strength was dried up as by the heat of
> > summer. *Selah*

Envy's sin unfolds into any number of sins: it blooms into violence, revenge in word and deed, and hurtful speech—accusatory, scornful, gossipy, and slanderous.

And the poem shows, too, how all kinds of sin bring others in. Gluttony is on his way to repentance when he takes down everyone in the tavern, or maybe they take him down. All that enfolding and refolding of allegory allows the individual person's sin to merge with something bigger, even more than a system, some force far beyond the symbolic. The failure to get beyond the sin seems to ultimately transform the individual, real-person characters into almost demonic figures of temptation that engage with the social system and the individual both.

Pastor and scholar Matt Croasmun uses emergence theory to describe the intertwined levels on which sin operates. Emergence theory helps him to think about how sins like racism plague American society. Croasmun says, "Race as a category seems to be constituted and maintained through multiple feedback loops of supervenience and downward causation. The consequences of racism, in turn, propagate in all directions: 'upward' from racist individuals to social institutions; 'downward' from those institutions to racialized actors; and even to the unconscious neurological activity within their brains, whence come psychological impulses not unrelated to racialized ideology. Accounts of culpability, simple within a reductionist framework, are complicated—and *expanded*."

Marvelously clear, his words, but reading them, I see the ways that I am not *less* responsible, but rather more. I've been reading the ledger over and over since grad school, with group after group of students, and the number never goes down. Croasmun's a pastor at a charismatic church; he knows there are more things in heaven and earth, Mercutio, so forth. It doesn't take away my culpability to say that whatever's emerging here is demonic.

In *No Name in the Street*, you call it "nightmare"—the sin of individuals, which is the sin of the Man, which is the structural sin, which is the emergent Thing. I remember gasping when I read it. When that white man sexually assaulted you, you were able to see his heinous act and its position in the social evil, the lack of connection at its root. You put that man's action into its emergent context/expression: "It is absolutely certain that white men, who invented the n[——]'s big black prick, are still at the mercy of the nightmare, and are still, for the most part, doomed, in one way or another, to attempt to make this prick their own: so much for the progress which the Christian world had made from that jungle in which it is their clear intention to keep black men treed forever."

When I want to do good, evil is right there with me. Day and night among the tombs, scratching himself—that man knew what the nightmare was about. He's here too, in the mirror, in the Hidden Five's hot, breathless graveyard.

In *Another Country*, when Cass, white woman, is talking to Ida, Black woman, about the racial ledger, it hits the reader just this same, breathtaking way.

> "Maybe," said Cass, with a sudden flash of anger, and very close to tears, "it happened to all of us! . . . Maybe we're worse off than you."
>
> "Oh," said Ida, "you are. There's no maybe about that."

Grass

"Then have a little mercy."
"You're asking a lot."

Mercy. Mercy.

Hardly a surprise for you, all the white people looking for absolution. It's so tedious and tiring. I can hardly do anything else, though I don't ask mercy of *you*, I guess. Or not only. If I say, *Son of David, have mercy on me, a sinner!*, I mean the both of you. From you, the truth that doesn't turn away from a fellow human. From the Other, that too, and more.

⟜

John Grimes in *Go Tell It on the Mountain* asked for it— mercy—when he was moaning his way to conversion on the threshing floor. He was passing through a night that juxtaposed his own coming of age struggles with the history of racial trauma and familial secret sin he couldn't have known. Surely his cry for mercy is a cry for mercy for all of it.

I lip the lines in *Piers Plowman*:

> Keep mercy in your mind and with your
> mouth beseech it.
> *His mercy is over all his works*, etc.
> And all the wickedness in this world that one
> could do or think
> Is no more to the mercy of God than a spark
> amid the sea! (V.281–83)

The line, the perfect, magical long line, that can work mercy itself into your mouth until you are bodily praying instead of bodily sinning. There is mercy in another line, mercy in keeping going, which is maybe why your books kept getting longer and longer and longer.

But mercy isn't what happens to John's father, Gabriel, in *Go Tell It on the Mountain* when he thinks he gets a sign of forgiveness for his adultery. As his wife, Deborah, and sister, Florence, both know, truth is necessary for the mercy to come. But Gabriel doesn't ever even admit the truth of his bloodguilt, of his abandonment of Esther and their son conceived in sin.

I know you're a great novelist because of how bad I feel for the villain Gabriel. You know what went into his making—and yet your work registers the mercy that comes from seeing more.

Gabriel couldn't admit the truth, and so he couldn't accomplish a restitution he longed to make.

> Thus it fares with such folk who follow all
> their will,
> Live evilly and don't leave off till life
> forsakes them.
> Dread rising from despair then drives
> away grace
> So that mercy may not come to their minds
> at that time;

Good hope that should help alters to
                wanhope—
Not from any impotence of God, as if he had
                not the power
To amend all that is amiss and his
                mercy greater
Than all our wicked works, as the Holy Writ
                witnesses:
   His mercy is above all his works—
But before his righteousness turns to ruth
                some restitution is needed;
His sorrow is satisfaction for such a one as
                may not pay. (XVII.311-20)

It's all in Zacchaeus, amen, who climbed that hunting stand, just there, across this hidden field, to see the kingdom come. Seeing Jesus, then being called by Jesus, he climbed down, ready to pay dues. "If I have defrauded anyone, I will give it back—four times as much." Maybe he had enough to pay that, but I doubt it. If I've learned anything from paycheck deductions and years of unions, it's this: dues aren't just collected; they're collective. No one can pay, and certainly not alone.

Easier said than done, though. "He lies drowned in dream," said Peace, "and so do many others."

I want you to know, James Baldwin, that when I write to you here, you dead, I don't want to make you some-

thing else, something other than you are. I'm not coun-
tering or glossing over any critique/problem you had with
the church. I read *The Fire Next Time*, and will continue
to, and will ask students to read it with me. And you get
to be whatever you in fact are, held in the Word, hid in
whatever life, whatever field, you are now. I'm not calling
you anything; I'm just calling you.

If you want to know why I thought I could call you
like this, by name, James Baldwin, I do have a reason.
This is it: whatever you believed, wherever you ended up,
you wrote me open in *Go Tell It on the Mountain* with the
line "John saw the Lord." Yes, I get that he saw the Lord
"for a moment only." But the darkness—yes, yes, "for a
moment only"—was, it *was*, "filled with a light." He *was*
"set free." Maybe I could be?

Tiffany

SEPTEMBER 6, 2020

Dear James Baldwin:

Woke up at 2:34 a.m. from a dream, the upshot of which
was "Set thy house in order, for thou shalt die, and not
live." I know why I dreamt it, from a psychological stand-
point. I've been reading your works one after the other,

your voice thundering in my ears while I move fences, and it's your dad's favorite verse.

But that's only part of it. My mother-in-law had also just been talking about one time when, while she was in the crawl space cleaning, she felt God speaking to her: it's time to sell the house. And how when driving one time, she'd heard from God too, to make final arrangements for her infirm sister. I'm sure these mixed and mingled in my mind to produce such a dream.

Memento mori is wise, and I tried to embrace it as calmly as possible. What seemed the worst thing was not the idea of death, exactly, for I have ideas about it. It was rather the sheer number of messes in my house that bothered me. It was a sense of inability, incapacity. I knew that the middle of the night is not precisely the time to set one's house in order, though I suppose one takes what one can get. How can I set anything in order? The mess—literal and figurative—is too big.

You said in a speech at Kalamazoo, "I conceive of my own life as a journey toward something I do not understand, which in the going toward, makes me better. I conceive of God, in fact, as a means of liberation and not a means to control others." You and *Go Tell It on the Mountain*'s John both, apparently.

But it can, on a bad day—and this is one of the bad days for me—be a bit more edgy to approach the Almighty. I don't care if it is. When Rufus in *Another Country* is dying, leaping off a bridge, when "he felt a shoe fly off behind him, [and] there was nothing around him, only the wind," he says, "*All right, you motherfucking Godalmighty bastard, I'm coming to you.*" As profound a confession of faith as I have ever heard.

Long ago, Mom asked: *Would you want to get chemo again if the cancer comes back? Or would you want to go to be with Jesus?* Nighttime thoughts.

I thought of the things people would need if I died—the will, which I still have not had people sign, even though I did a free internet version; the passwords; insurance; the promised college tuition benefit for the children. And to not have to clean out my skeletons in the attic.

In other news of impending doom, the election is coming. A big debate about billboards on the Town Forum Facebook page—some people had raised money to put up a Black Lives Matter billboard on a lonely stretch of Route 20 on the way west out of town. Opponents then raised money for MANY Blue Lives Matter billboards and Support Local Business billboards, which had pretty much the same message with different words. The town itself weighed in, hoisting blue-line banners from the light posts—not just on Main Street either, but down a side street where Kendra would have let her Black sons ride their bikes like the other children, if she dared, which she doesn't.

At the bowling alley on Wednesdays, we can do yoga at 6:30 p.m. and hear the blues at 7. Neighbors will call at midnight when our dog's out, saying don't worry, Louise is safe in the garage and we gave her a treat. But with these flags and banners and billboards, it looks like the sundown town it let itself be. A group gathered by the billboards to take pictures and post them on Facebook.

All this business doesn't get to me only. Kendra and Terry are stressed. They have trouble sleeping. They type out comments to reply to ignorant posts, then sometimes delete them. It messes with family dynamics. Terry said to me, diplomatically, "I wish people would read more." None of the majority-white town citizens has to think about any of the things he has to think about. They would find his experiences shocking, hard to believe, or at best, bewildering. You knew—Americans "have a very deep-seated distrust of real intellectual effort (probably because we suspect that it will destroy, as I hope it does, that myth of America to which we cling so desperately)."

One of the kids on the Citizens for Equality Facebook page decided we needed another march. He cleared it with the police and received permission to walk from the middle school parking lot down the main route through town and onto State Street to the little park to the pavil-ion. As the date—yesterday now—approached, the Forum got more and more heated, the talk of guns and violence more emphatic.

The day of the march, it was clear to even my husband, who was determined to stay out of things like this, that he needed to be with us. Given that he wasn't much of a "sun's out, guns out," Second Amendment–defender type, he probably wouldn't be able to *protect* us, but presence isn't nothing. He's tall, farmer-strong.

It was on the one hand completely pathetic. There were maybe fifteen marchers when we got to the parking lot at the middle school, possibly fewer. And Terry, who'd waved his giant Black Lives Matter flag last time, and Kendra, who'd brought her family last time, didn't seem to be there. It was all set to be another cheesy white liberal conscience comforter that does nothing. But there were police in the parking lot too—a lot of them.

Police on every corner, and police at the final destination, which seemed like a not insignificant expenditure for the force in town, in a small town where a good deal of the tax levy goes toward police. I wore my "The Church Will Not Be Silent" shirt with a long skirt, dressed the kids up. "Martin Luther King dressed up for marches. It demands respect," I told them. A politics of respectability, maybe, for both King and us, but still. I could FEEL the police officers' attempts to create goodwill, in their nods, and their respectful demeanor toward us, which is another difference between my experience and yours.

All along the route, there were large pickup trucks with swaths of gargantuan Trump and Blue Lives Matter flags. Engines of passing cars revved at the stoplight. Someone had even found an old-school *hearse* and was driving it back and forth, back and forth along the route. The children talked—Fiona with the organizer, about the church's scriptural grounds for resistance against racial injustice, and Beckett with me, sharing snarky, podcast-inspired remarks toward the honkers.

When we passed by the insurance agency in town, there was not any longer a B, L, or M crayoned into the window. There was, however, an extremely respectfully dressed older man with a tiny, neatly hand-lettered sign that said, "Black Lives Matter Is a Communist Organization." His voice had the Father-forgive-them tone, so gentle and pleading.

The park, where the march was to end, was the showdown square. There were trucks all around, trucks that didn't belong to the marchers and which seemed to be there mostly for intimidation purposes. Someone with small children and a swanky minivan had brought a cooler of bottled waters to support the marchers—she couldn't bring her children to the march itself in case things got violent, she said, but she wanted to do what she could.

Terry and Kendra showed up at the end there in the pavilion, in a sort of weary posture of doing their duty. They said they'd been driving around, seeing what was happening, and decided that the muscle show was enough. They brought with them that same Black Lives Matter flag again—one flag against many.

The scene had the air of everyone waiting for something to go down, the air of everyone being ready to be ready for something to go down. Both the tiny size of the group of marchers and the nature of the antics of those opposing the march seemed ridiculous.

I reminded myself that situations like this were absurd enough to become dangerous—*had* on any number of occasions become dangerous. I reminded myself to pray during the minutes of silence.

After it was over, we walked everyone back to their cars, "by another route," as it were, for safety. We cut through the Lutheran church parking lot. A very nice man was coming out of what must have been the cleanup after a Saturday evening service.

"Coming back from the march?" he asked. "How did it go?"

Some vague, positive comments.

"And did you talk to many people?"

Galling question, James Baldwin, but a good one. As far as I could tell, no one had talked to *anyone* on the other side—except my husband and the photographer, who, not deigning to march, just accompanied, behind and to the side.

I was reading an article about you in the *Paris Review*, one of those writer interviews that they do. You said there was a reason you felt you needed to be involved in the civil rights movement, in the sit-ins and things, even though Ralph Ellison thought you shouldn't, that it wasn't your vocation. What was that reason? Spokesman? Witness? Interpreter? What's the writer to do?

Grass

Today made me think of that famous moment that everyone cites from *No Name*: your arrival at the Montgomery Airport, when you saw those John Wayning white men hostilely eyeing you out of the building: "And if the eyes of those men had had the power to pulverize that car, it would have been done, exactly as, in the Bible, the wicked city is leveled—I had never in all my life seen such a concentrated, malevolent poverty of spirit."

But am I the only one who hears Jesus when you say that phrase, "poverty of spirit"? Surely not. You must have known when you wrote that, what it would mean for you to allude to the Sermon on the Mount, the poor in spirit and the kingdom of heaven Jesus promises them. By which I mean for all of us—whatever side—at that march.

I told one of my colleagues about the demonstration and how I was interpreting your allusion, and he said, well, yes, but don't miss that Baldwin called it "malevolent" poverty of spirit. Meaning that you weren't calling this sort of poverty of spirit the good kind, not a BE-attitude. I have no problem with that reading, the important judgment. But isn't malevolence at least one of the conditions that the revelation of the kingdom, the revelation of the Lord, is *for*?

⌐

Did you ever used to sing that song we used to sing at tent meetings?

Jesus on the mainline, tell him what you want.
You just call him up, and tell him what you
want, what you want.
If you're sick and you want to get well . . .
If you need a miracle . . .
If you need the Holy Ghost . . .

Dead in our transgressions, I guess, walking in the Hidden Five. Our sins sound like a ravening pack of coyotes when they get to howling. Call him up. Call him up.

I want the kingdom, James Baldwin—not the keys to it only. I want it on earth as it is in heaven. I want Jesus to loose the bonds of injustice, to undo the thongs of the yoke, to let the oppressed go free, and to break every yoke. I want us to be satisfied in the parched places, to be like watered gardens, to dance. And I want us, here, to be called the repairer of the breach. I am calling from the Hidden Five in the dark.

From across the field, our dog Louise barks back.

⟿

When you described the writer as specially equipped for "the endeavor to wed the vision of the Old World with that of the New" in "The Discovery of What It Means to Be an American," you were talking about Europe and America. But you mostly called the vision of a better

America by other names—achieving our country, the welcome table, the New Jerusalem, a kind of resurrection and transformation that brings "the hope of liberation." You insisted that "the intangible dreams of people have a tangible effect on the world."

At the height of this pandemic surge my imaginary Hidden Five graveyard would be full of bodies before noon on the second day. Burial after burial—one every thirty seconds or so, and getting faster and faster. By now, death has undone very, very many. Day and night, I wander in the Hidden Five among the tombs. I think to myself, if I just stay with the sheep, I won't hurt anyone. I will get less benefit from being a white woman; I will be doing my work, and no one will know how little love animates it. I am sitting in the field, just the dead burying the dead in the wind, with the unceasing sound of the road behind.

> And a whirring wakes me from my wildness
> and I startle to see and hear a corporeal hiss,
> a vast, gasping, grown-great multitude
> of dry grasshoppers humming to
> > human shape
> blown of scant breeze, brown bodies brittle—
> and the rattle of sandy thistle grass
> > their reveille.
> All around the wind was white fear, words

broken off, bereft of breath.
As the wind rose, their wan rasps rankled
and one by one they fell and sank into the
    grassy sea.
Those were eyes, those were pearls, those
    were treasure
buried in the field. We had buried them,
    burdened,
in the Hidden Five.

And comes a glint in the dark graveyard of the field—a woman, alive, Pilate Dead from Toni Morrison's *Song of Solomon*. There is a light like a star from her earring, a dangling brass snuffbox with words curled inside. Pilate is walking the tall grass among the tombs, and her coming sounds the susurrus, breath over the breathless.

"My baby girl." A stirring and another "My baby girl." Then another *shush* and "That's my baby girl." "My baby girl." "My baby girl." She combs through the grasses, thistles, alfalfa, bottlebrush spikes, like fingers through hair, calling each one from the grave, "My baby. My baby. That's my baby."

And then, as if the words were unfurled from the lit glint of her ear-box itself, and the flame were tongue and sun, comes a sung note, a surge. And she is singing, "Mercy"—her word a note held, soft, tentative, cradled in a hand. And she takes a breath, and say-sings it again, opening outward, like petals, like this little light.

And from beside her comes a humming from the dark. At first, it is as if the sound of the road were in the field. But it is a man, alive, an ancient man, C. C. Miller, beekeeper, who built our house. His beard, bizarre, fringes across his chin, hides all except his voice. He finds the beginning of breath, as if in the beginning bellow of a small church's organ—and out comes a buzzing harmony with her, as if across the teeth of a wax-papered comb. Mercy on the *m*, the hum deep in his throat the sound of bees in the box in the cellar on a too-warm night. He hums with Pilate Dead, like people in prayer do when they agree. But then they are singing, their mouths opening, the two together one.

The brown-black dark grass of night springs up as from a sudden gust. The sky mauves, and the trees sharpen, and the east is coals breathed on by bellows.

Then comes Christ—from among the foreign pines, striding into this field. And he is crowned in oak and linden, his arms pitched wide, bared, at the angles of the road. And when he steps into the field, the box on Pilate Dead's ear opens, and it is books, and the words emerge and fly to him. And from C. C. Miller's throat, from his open mouth, come swarms of bees, straight to Christ's dripping fingers, to the flowers of his crown.

And Jesus says, "This grass shall live!"

The sound of his mouth wrapping around the *r* of the grass greens it. And the crack echo of the *live live live live live* sounds real reveille to every single baby, every dead and buried flower seed.

The sheep bolted the fence at the crack and raced into the woods. I followed them, running, the tree branches slapping my face.

On the way back through the forest, in the early morning light of God's honest truth, I saw a stem of Queen Anne's lace, upright and strong, with my pretentious pen hanging on.

Tiffany

3

Forest

In our fields, fallow and burdened, in grass and furrow,
In barn and stable, with scythe, flail, or harrow,
Sheepshearing, milking or mowing, on labour that's older
Than knowledge, with God we work shoulder to shoulder;
God providing, we dividing, sowing, and pruning;
Not knowing yet and yet sometimes discerning:
Discerning a little at Spring when the bud and shoot
With pointing finger show the hand at the root,
With stretching finger point the mood in the sky:
Sky and root in joint action; and the cry
Of the unsteady lamb allying with the brief
Sunlight, with the curled and cautious leaf.

—Christopher Fry, *The Boy with a Cart*

Janie saw her life like a great tree in leaf with the things suffered,
things enjoyed, things done and undone. Dawn and doom was in
the branches.

—Zora Neale Hurston, *Their Eyes Were Watching God*

*A*t one time, long ago, the forest where we live in northern Illinois was an oak savanna with a great deal more light. The land was wide, giving quarter to tall bluestem, milkweed, black-eyed Susan, and the majesty was in the grasses—yes, Lord—and the oaks. The oaks held everything around them, as sheltering hens; even the thunderous ruminants plagued by flies deigned to pause in their shade.

I have to kind of piece it together from what I see here now.

But I think about how it was, open country, oaks glory-twisting like the grass around them.

Those oaks welcomed flame, kept it sacred, like the Potawatomi, cradled it, and let it go. They were consumed, yes, but also made new, flowering into acorn fruits. They were limbed for wind, like they didn't even mind.

⌐

I may have been destined for the woods. In 1995, I was writing my high school graduation speech. Most of the public speaking I'd heard was sermons, and I needed a text, turn-with-me-if-you-will. This was public school, though, not church, so instead of John 3:16, I chose American children's literature: Shel Silverstein's *The Giving Tree*. It was a pick full of nostalgia for Mrs. Linda Piddock's first-grade read-alouds, but for me worth full interpretive attention.

The Giving Tree begins with a tree and a boy, full of affection and play. But the boy turns to other pursuits. And the tree loves the boy so much that she tries to help him toward his pursuits by letting him lop off parts of her. When he's young and greedy, she surrenders her fruit to sell for cash. When he wants human relationships, she lets him saw off her corona of branches for a house. When it all goes south, she offers even her great trunk to his ax so that he can make a canoe and escape all his sorrows.

The tree loves to give to the boy when he comes to her, but she's stripped and diminished by his taking. Yet she apologizes when the boy, now a stooped old man, returns one more time. And even then, she finds something, because the tired-out old boy needs a place to sit and rest. She ends the book happy, finally, because again, she has something to give—and because again, they are together.

My choice of *The Giving Tree* for the speech was a little odd. Dr. Seuss's *Oh, the Places You'll Go!* was the preferred graduation text that year, or, if you were going old-school, then Robert Frost's "The Road Not Taken." But it was in keeping with my sermonic aims—maybe even a latent vocation to preach.

Even though I went to public school, possibly because I went to public school, I planned to bear witness to the gospel, at this, my last chance to connect with my whole class. And, too, I wanted to respond to the sorts of things people said at graduations—about what we should do: things about places one will go, about roads taken and not.

To do these things, I offered a passionate though truly dubious reading of the text in which the tree can be viewed as a sacrificial Christ. Christ was the real giving tree and we the giving trees that would be.

I believed in giving; or anyway, I talked about it all the time. In heady days of camp ministry during college, I had shared with the staff my life hope that I would always give, rather than take. I even got a letter one time from one of my coworkers, an end-of-summer goodbye: "I want you to know that I have a lot of respect for you," he wrote, "and confidence that you will live the full life of a giver." His letter was written on birch bark.

At my wedding, instead of 1 Corinthians 13, I had them read Philippians 2, because of the sacrifice implied.

> Do nothing from selfish ambition or empty conceit,
> but in humility regard others as better than your-
> selves. Let each of you look not to your own interests

but to the interests of others. Let the same mind be in you that was in Christ Jesus,

> who, though he existed in the form of God,
> did not regard equality with God
> as something to be grasped,
> but emptied himself,
> taking the form of a slave,
> assuming human likeness.
> And being found in appearance as a human,
> he humbled himself
> and became obedient to the point of death—
> even death on a cross.

See? Giving and a tree.

Here in the forest, *The Giving Tree* reads differently. I confess to being a bit confused. *Should* the tree have done all that giving, all of herself like that? That *does* seem to be what is asked of all the *shes* in the world. And even if we assume yes on that question, what does that sacrifice even accomplish for the boy? We see no evidence that her gifts actually get him the money, house, family, or lasting satisfaction that he seeks. All that giving up—what difference does it make?

Or what about the boy? What IS the tree to him? Is she the tree of life? If so, then he should take and eat. Or is it the tree of the knowledge of good and evil? If so, then he should neither take nor eat, though if he does, he may gain at tragic cost a certain sour experience and knowledge.

Forest

And if he's playing king of the forest, what kind of king is he who would cut down his own, his only, subject?

⌒

In 2017, as we prepared to move to the forest, Kristen Page, an ecologist friend of mine, visited it with me. We walked through the fierce, freezing wind of the soy fields into the scrub and trees. It was the most passable part of the year for a forest thickly briared most of the time. It was unleaved, and we might see. I worried that I'd get us lost.

And, too, I felt like some mother fretting over a beloved but bedraggled child. There were so many brambles, falling trees, invading honeysuckle bushes. The hirsute gooseberry scraped at our legs and Virginia stickseed tacked strands of burrs over our winter coats. There was also an enormous, ancient rusted cultivator, a million beer cans, and even a fake open grave with a fake human skeleton.

We'd heard that sometime in the last twenty years, someone had come in with some kind of machinery and cleared out a dirt track back in there. That explained the overgrown clearing we got through to. It also explained why we walked past enough tires for a used car lot, sometimes in patterned groups, sometimes with a tree growing up through their middles: they must have been obstacles for the bikes to clear.

Kristen looked at the trees. This is basswood, she said, this elm; these are oaks—all these, walnut trees.

She crouched down and told me about the differences between red oak acorns and black oak acorns: one has its cap pulled down farther than the other. She pointed to a bulbous growth that occurs on some goldenrod stalks— there's a worm in there, she said, and chickadees like to eat it. You'll see a little hole when they peck it out.

We walked into a three-season pondish area that was slowly killing the thick old trees in its midst. "I might not let the kids play in this part of the forest on windy days like this," she said, looking around again.

But then she said, "This is a good woods."

I was thinking of recent pressures on us to log the woods, of cantankerous scrapping about how we might pay the taxes on land deemed by the town recreational, about where to get money to pay for the orchard that Josh dreamed of. Walnut, he'd said, is valuable. And besides, if we took some out, there would be more light for the oaks, more room for the trees we want to plant. But how could we cut down hundred-year-old trees, even if the land *was* more properly oak savanna?

I said, "What we're struggling with, though, is what to do with it. I mean, how do we take care of it? What should we do?"

She looked around again. "You should get to know it," she said.

In George Eliot's *Middlemarch*, Dorothea wants only to know and to do what is right. Having at her disposal a good fortune, she wonders how best to give it away so that she might accomplish the most good. She wants to help others—she sketches cottages for poor people in her free time. She gives up jewelry, pet dogs, even riding because all may not share in its pleasures.

"She likes giving up," her sister, Celia, says.

"If that were true, Celia, my giving-up would be self-indulgence, not self-mortification," Dorothea replies.

According to Bert G. Hornback, the "beauty and life" of *Middlemarch* emerge from its energetic defense of the ideas that "to help others is good; to sacrifice oneself for the sake of others is grand, noble, and heroic." Sacrifice seems like the most trustworthy path to goodness and meaningful action.

But which sacrifice, which good? "What could she do, what ought she to do?" Dorothea asks again and again and again.

As Dorothea considers marriage to Mr. Casaubon—an ill-equipped scholar on a wild goose chase for the key to all mythologies—she thinks that it will "deliver her from her girlish subjection to her own ignorance." The narrator tells us of Dorothea that "the thing which seemed to her best, she wanted to justify by the completest knowledge."

Now, it might be my religious background in reading, but that wording seems to identify Dorothea's decision tree with the tree of the knowledge of good and evil. She is certainly drawn away by her own desires and enticed.

> "I should learn everything [if married to Casaubon]," she said to herself, still walking quickly along the bridle road through the wood. "It would be my duty to study that I might help him the better in his great works. There would be nothing trivial about our lives. Everyday-things with us would mean the greatest things. It would be like marrying Pascal. I should learn to see the truth by the same light as great men have seen it by. And then I should know what to do, when I got older: I should see how it was possible to live *a grand life* here—now—in England."

We watch Dorothea take the fruit of knowledge in Casaubon's offer of marriage, surrendering ultimately the relative freedom of singleness in a trade for a certain knowledge of what she should do. That is to say, Dorothea takes on the constraints of marriage so that someone else has the responsibility of limning out her proper, sacrificial duty and attaching it to meaningfulness in life.

Of course, Dorothea, nicknamed Dodo by her sister, gets from Casaubon neither knowledge nor meaningful self-sacrifice. Indeed, even when she remarries the gorgeous young Will Ladislaw in a love match at the end, Dorothea never stops "feeling that there was always something better which she might have done, if she had only been better and known better."

Though Dorothea "never repent[s] that she had given up position and fortune to marry Will Ladislaw," readers feel no less the bittersweetness of her life of "beneficent activity which she had not the doubtful pains of discovering and marking out for herself." The hospital she had planned to fund with her inheritances never comes to fruition. And no cottages for poor people are built after all.

Critics have had varied responses to Dorothea's self-sacrifice that reflect, of course, the patriarchy. The *Saturday Review* asserted that "surely it is not every girl's duty to refuse the advantages and pleasures of the condition in which she finds herself because all do not share them. She is not selfish because she is serenely happy in a happy home; and if she does her best to help and alleviate the suffering within her reach, she may comfort herself in the belief that the eye of Providence never sleeps."

I guess. Maybe only "a *man's* reach should exceed his grasp"?

Leslie Stephen groused that "Dorothea was content with giving [Will] 'wifely help'; asking his friends to dinner, one supposes, and copying his ill-written manuscripts. Many lamented that 'so rare a creature should be absorbed into the life of another,' though no one could point out exactly what she ought to have done. That is just the pity of it. There was nothing for her to do; and I can only comfort myself by reflecting that, after all, she had a dash of stupidity, and that more successful Theresas may do a good deal of mischief."

I suppose we are all wondering what we ought to do.

My students on a study abroad trip to England would have agreed with Stephen. They mostly laughed at Dorothea's vocational confusion. They even counted the number of times she rushed to a window and sobbed about it all—a lot: it became a trip joke. My defenses of Dorothea were feeble. What could I say but that I found myself lost in the woods with her sometimes too?

But one afternoon, a woman in my class asked me to go on a walk with her. We wandered east into the yard of St. Mary and St. John Church in East Oxford. It was thickly treed and overgrown with many perennial wildflowers—a space right for reflection. It even had its own Trinity labyrinth in the brickwork, which felt just right for *Middlemarch*, a book obsessed with labyrinthine imagery. We peered at the graves: carpenters, tailors, organ builders, workhouse staff, bricklayers, mental health nurses, public health inspectors, cattle dealers, war dead, teachers, and many, many children. It felt an astonishing turn—off from Cowley Road with its fast-paced businesses. It seemed far away, too, from the more formally ordered and grandiose Oxford colleges with their martyrs and great scholars.

My walking partner was the only married student on the trip, finishing up her last undergraduate credits abroad before she and her husband moved far away together into their new life. She liked the book a lot, she told me—especially the way it portrayed marriage. That's almost all we said on the whole long walk through those dense trees, separated only by graves.

⟿

On what became the forest where we live, networks of trade and cultural exchange existed far before white settlers planted themselves. Kiikaapoi (Kickapoo), Sauk and Meskwaki (Sac and Fox), Myaamia (Miami), Hoocąk (Ho-Chunk), Očhéthi Šakówiŋ (Sioux), and Bodwéwadmi (Potawatomi) moved, resided, planted, fought, and made peace, managing relations with other tribes, encroaching settlers, and emerging national powers. In the early nineteenth century, the Potawatomi had seasonal settlements in the area I drive most days.

It definitely wasn't how William Cullen Bryant said it was when he visited Princeton, Illinois, just ninety miles from here in 1832 and wrote "The Prairies"—"All [Indian culture] is gone; / All—save the piles of earth that hold their bones." The disappearing Indian was a powerful and common poetic image, but it downplays the extent to which tribes in the broader region worked out their sovereign responses to the genocidal injustice of the Indian Removal Act of 1830. These involved both going and staying, sometimes a bit of both. In a problematic treaty in 1804—problematic since it had been enacted by Sac and Fox tribal members without authority to negotiate the treaty and because it did not achieve proper compensation—the Sac and Fox ceded to the United States the land on which we make our farm. In a later treaty, in 1833, the Chippewa, Ottawa, and Potawatomi ceded their rights to it. The Pokagon band of Potawatomi in western Michigan and northern Indiana stayed—they still assert and defend tribal rights to the Chicago lakefront. But other members of the Potawatomi would leave north central Indiana through central Illinois in what came to be known as the Trail of Death in 1838.

There were provisos in the 1833 agreement, however, that non-Native settlers refrain from settling until late 1836. Potawatomi in this area planned one last spring planting that year, but white settlers had come before the deadline. Right around the corner from where we live, William Hamilton of Ohio treated the Potawatomi, who'd wintered elsewhere, as already removed and disappeared, plundering their summer residences of bark and copper pots as if the dwellings had been abandoned. The copper pots were reportedly reclaimed, but the bark, already incorporated into new dwellings, seems to have been given up by the Indigenous folks. Not sure how they could have gotten it back.

The local historian Ed Urban writes that from the documents we have of local history, Potawatomi tribal members' "departure is not documented; but one thing is for certain—Hamilton didn't see them leave. He died that spring in 1836 from an injury that he sustained the previous fall. He was injured by a falling timber, while helping Calvin Spencer, the founder of the town, build a log structure."

Fields wrestled the savanna into squares, plows, houses. In the middle part of the nineteenth century, settlers planted orchards here, with ash-leaf maple for building protection and Osage orange for hedgerows. And other things: honeysuckle and multiflora roses—both vehemently invasive and the roses painfully prickling, with great, spreading, vicious sprawls of spines.

⟶

My getting lost in the labyrinthine woods started our first full day there: February of 2017. I came up with the kids to do some cleaning before we moved in, because the house smelled like a family of squirrels lived in its crevices, which, in fact, was the case. Josh was at a farmer's market for his internship job.

I sent the children out to explore the forest while I tackled the indoor stench with vinegar and soap and water. I thought I could rely on the kids fighting, if nothing else, to keep me apprised of their position, which it did for a while. But then I lost track of them. Then I was wandering in the woods, calling Beckett's name. And then a neighbor we'd just met, Geoff, was looking for Beckett too, and Fiona was looking also, closer to the house. And then I was bellowing myself hoarse across a frozen hell of leafless prickers, burdock, and stickseeds, leaping over downed logs, forcing my way through. Naturally, my phone was nearly dead.

I couldn't find him because he was truly lost—and so was I, of course. What did I know of this large forest? Certainly not where it or we would end up.

Our neighbor told me later how scared he was that day. Here he was, the potentially creepy neighbor who lives alone next door and the kid disappears. He'd called the police, he told me. He'd never been, he told me, so scared in his life.

"I got out my pistol."

That brought me up short. Both of us in the forest, running and shouting for the lost boy. And him with a gun tucked somewhere—all that panicked, pressurized time.

A group of disc golfers found Beckett crying in the park woods that abuts our land—and they called the police too. We got to ride home in the police car—whether the police the neighbor called or the police the golfers called, I don't know. We hardly knew how to tell the officer where our house even was, me babbling in relief, having no road names to speak of yet, no landmarks, and not enough phone battery to fuel a consultation with Google.

I'd never known there was no padding in the back of a police car. It was all hard plastic, the seats like scooped-out school chairs. There was neither anything for comfort nor anything with which to make a weapon.

"The weirdest thing to me," our neighbor Geoff said, "was that after it was over, when you guys came back in the police car, you just went straight back to work."

Forest

⌐⌐

In 1856, C. C. Miller, a doctor and musician from Pennsylvania, transplanted himself to the town here. He gave up medicine soon after he arrived, having had great anxiety about that vocation, if he should hurt someone in a career that was trying to do good. He tried out several things after that—traveling sheet music sales, musical instruction, the principalship of several local high schools. In 1857, he married a widow, Helen M. White, "a woman," he wrote, "of remarkable energy and executive ability." In 1858, he built the house where I live now.

On July 5, 1861, while he was away in Chicago, Helen White Miller saw a swarm of bees hanging in the air over the front porch. Such a mystery—the still swarm in the air—would have appeared to a woman of such energy and ability as the gift it was. She knocked the bees into a full-size sugar barrel and turned it hive. This she did at great personal cost: she seems to have had localized swelling-rash reactions to five or six stings during the swarm. These sent her to bed—and she could thereafter participate in the bee enterprise she inaugurated only "in a case of extremity."

But she had captured the vocation of her man. It took him six years to turn a profit, but he became the biggest honey producer on the continent. He planted rows of linden and fields of clover, documented plants, and redesigned hive boxes. And he wrote book after book: *A Year with the Bees, Forty Years with the Bees, Fifty Years with the Bees*.

When he died, the Beekeepers Association's national meeting made a caravan from Madison to the house where I live. They set a plaque for C. C. Miller in the local Presbyterian church—the one where I preach sometimes. They had lunch on the lawn with the second Mrs. Miller, Sidney, whom C. C. Miller had married after Helen's death.

The walnut trees in the forest where we live advanced everywhere, seeping juglone poison, winning every competition for soil and light. Their straight, parallel panels of leaves blocked other vegetation from the light. Their trunks grew for a hundred years, preparing, one might presume, to become straight floorboards that gleam darkness.

Walnut fruit falls on the forest floor or into the crotch of some honeysuckle by a smash through leaves—fast, in a kind of cymbal crash, a bounce from boughs. It accelerates as it goes, but it's all over, pretty much, in a second, and the moment I hear its traveling is when I realize what has happened.

This is just to say, when a walnut falls, I hear the time passing. I might have, I think to myself, predicted what was going to happen, as if I could hear the inevitability of the fall. It is at hand, the green gone soon in a glop of yellow amber that darkens to wood stain on skin.

Forest

Prodigious, the forest, fearsome in fecundity. The whole place has gone *Sleeping Beauty*, the part before the kissing prince when the land grows wild in a hundred-year isolation. A No Trespassing sign is less warning than observation: arching black raspberry canes trip all comers, innumerable burdocks scourge, multiflora rose tooths through denim—these are enough to keep people away.

Time's principle is scarcity, but the forest is not scarce.

⌒

We decided to pasture animals in the woods: pigs the first year, then goats, and now sheep. This year, due to the pandemic and my husband's long-hauler case of it, I have been the primary shepherd, feeding the sheep with invasive honeysuckle and wild grapevines as fodder. I move the flock through the woods with portable electric net fences that make them daily pastures. They've been nearly four months in the woods as we try to save the open fields from overgrazing and try to rescue forest ground-cover from the overwhelming shade of honeysuckle.

Mornings, I lop for an hour or two early. I wrench off giant boughs bright with berries, climbing up to cut them, sometimes, or levering my weight or ribs against the loppers. I drag down, too, garlands of wide, yellowing grape leaves, some with purple clusters. The sheep crowd around me, moving wherever I chop, nosing past me into the green.

Each strand of the electric netting for the mobile sheep pasture comes to forty-eight paces. Every six or seven steps is a post, and eight posts makes a strand. These, when clutched, are actually too much to fit even a large-handed woman's clasp, so I scoop them up in both arms. We have seven lengths of fence, so the sheep travel in a leapfrog way, each day moving from one three- or four-length area to another. Yesterday's three lengths make the new pasture for today.

Here's how it works. First, I walk into the super-dense, overgrown area of the forest, counting my steps to find a path through that will be the right length so that the net can make a circuit abutting the sheep's current pasture. It usually takes me a few passes to find the right route, stomping down prickly gooseberry; I have gotten lost quite regularly. When I figure out where I am, I use the loppers to clear a sort of pathway.

Then I gather up a length of yesterday's fence. I pull up each post by wiggling it back and forth, and bundle it into my arms. As I do, moving along the fence length, the net catches bits of yesterday's cut-down, eaten-to-sticks honeysuckle and snags, stopping me and dragging the gathered net out and disarranging it. Spikes on the posts get woven into the net too, and I stop to uncatch the net from whatever. I try and pick up the full arm-load of netting to minimize the snags, but doing so re-arranges the spikes even more, thrusting them deep into the netted wires.

When I finally get the bundle to the path I have cut, I begin to unfold the net strand, stake by stake, which usually involves a great deal of detangling, as the net has gathered twigs on the journey and it tangles more as it unfurls. The second strand is usually slightly more difficult, as it needs to go past the first strand, another hazard, to its place.

When I move and set the third strand, I am damp, my shirt and Kevlar chaps are covered with burrs, the mosquitoes have found the spots where my garments may have shifted during transport. I am possibly swearing and/or crying, most certainly praying in emphatic tones, possibly with dramatic imprecations and thoughts about the other work I am not able to be doing.

I have to go back over the fence then, clip the strands together, pull the net taut, and walk it down so there are no gaps between the net and the ground that a sheep might want to get through if she gets bored of the fodder. Then I use the sledgehammer to wiggle the grounding rod until I can heave it out of the soil around the old pasture, move the sixty-pound marine battery, energizer, water bucket, and mineral bucket, pound in the grounding rod at the new spot, set up the clips on the battery and fence and rod, test the fence, and let the sheep slip through.

I let them eat for a few hours to transform the lower density of raspberry and gooseberry and young honeysuckle into a passable openness, where light might—and where the forest flowers, early spring beauty and Solomon's seal, might—have a chance next year. Later in the day, I come back with the loppers for another hour or two, hop the fence, and begin painstakingly hacking down the tree-sized honeysuckle bushes for their next meal.

I have wandered thus through my sabbatical, seeking hours to write between work in the forest every day, dragging a notebook with me.

This past winter, I read *Walden*—just *Walden*—with a group of students for eight weeks. I would come to class heady from just-born lambs I'd delivered myself, weary from every-two-hour feedings of Immortal Diamond, our recovering kitchen lamb. I'd show them pictures, and we'd show each other intricate journal entries that pored over *Walden*'s lines. It was rich and intimate, conversations focusing so closely on the text that we'd even consider its punctuation, then pulling back out again to examine ourselves as *Walden*'s readers.

Still, it was odd. It was maybe the most sustained experience of close reading I'd ever had with students, and they persisted in hating the object of our attention. Hating it as charitably as they could, of course.

We were four and a half weeks in, working through "The Ponds." It's a matchless, extended description of Walden Pond in all waters and lights and weathers, from every vantage and glint and in every glaze of sun or cloud beam. I was there, fully present, delighted. But just then, one woman burst out, as if she'd been holding in something for a long time.

She said, think of the hours he just was sitting there in the woods, looking at the lake. I mean, can you really justify that time? It's not an unfair question.

⤳

I mean, sometimes it's quite pleasant work, here in the woods. I open the sky. The crack, the fall of honeysuckle, and there it is: light again all the way to the forest floor. Now it can reach the oaks that would be, the daisy-headed fleabane, the pink lantern of phlox, and the Drummond's aster who takes her time.

And too, there are the sheep. I place my hands on their boned fur heads, rub around their ears, except for Spot, who doesn't like her head touched. These sheep are getting fat here, in the dense woods in the late summer, through the fall. I mean them all blessing and receive blessings upon blessings in return.

It does get to me, though, just how big a task it all is. The other day, I made Beckett come help me for an hour. The pasture had come round to one of those special areas of the forest where there was a huge cache of abandoned nursery plant pots and trays, broken grow lights, plastic bags full of what I can only assume were rabbit cage liners and shavings. I started us piling usable pots to save and tossing the broken pieces into the trash bags. Beckett wasn't having it, though: "This is impossible! Useless!"

I'm not sure how wrong he is. Most of the honeysuckle will return next year unless it is very cold this winter: it is first to arrive in the spring, last to unleave in fall. It will be years before what I am doing helps. Even the park district uses poison on honeysuckle. "It's like this," the wonderful head of volunteers said when we went one Saturday. "I don't want to use the herbicide—I have a degree in ecology. But one application, and it won't come back for a hundred years. I'd like to use goats, but we can't manage the flock, and it takes forever."

She wasn't lying, and the time it takes to shepherd the sheep also competes with other good things. The children, lonely with the COVID-loneliness, are getting sadder and sadder. And the suffering of the world's people and the injustice perpetrated by our government and our social order are by no means far from our local context.

I sharpen my loppers and pray for everything: for the sheep; for Thy kingdom come; for the land to heal; for the mattering God grants to make good. I think of Jesus, who taught all day and spent the nights in the forest on the Mount of Olives, who, when it came down to it, didn't want to make the sacrifice he'd purposed in his heart as the only way forward. At the key moment, he knelt down in a grove of trees to pray. "Not my will" seems important.

Forest

⟞⟶

One afternoon in the forest, I heard, from far away near the barn, our rooster crow. A magnificent bird, like a rainbow made of night-dark. He is iridescent, badass in that way that roosters are—weathered and almost wounded-looking. His black mass is fringed over by coppery fronds, bangs of the redhead with green between them.

You have to watch him, though. If he figures you're messing with him as you haul the heavy water buckets or scoop the feed, he won't scruple to jump you. There and then, his whole body becomes a darting arrow you should have seen coming.

There must have been some threat to make him call like that. Hearing him, I cast my mind on all the complaints in my mind, the attitudes, the bitterness—any number of betrayals.

⟞⟶

Wind is the only thing I fear, living in the woods. Many stormy nights I have to practice breathing techniques and work to not imagine the linden splitting and crushing through our home front and killing our children.

One day last summer, a storm came on when I was cutting down honeysuckle while Beckett and my dad played catch in a nearby semiclearing. The wind was rising, and as we were in the old part of the forest, I started to get nervous. Just as I called my father and Beckett to go in—too dangerous—a massive eighty-year-old tree let go, ripping across the forestscape and becoming a smoke cloud of sawdust against the ground. We were ten feet, fifteen tops, from where it landed; we smelled woodshop for days, a smell that said it could all come crashing down at any moment.

Maybe if I could describe all this work differently, I could make it mean something. I could talk about how today in the forest, I lured back the escaped sheep, shaking a yogurt container of grain-free dog food, swaying my hips with a herd of them behind me. In so doing, I drew not only the animals but also my husband behind me. Surely he must be by this very dance assured above all things that I am giving up so much for him and his dream.

Or, I could make it a funny story at a dinner party. I could describe the buffoonery of an animal escape. It goes like this: We find out about the escape and I jam my legs into khakis already covered in mud, which had been left in the bathroom for this very purpose. Then I spring out to the escaped mammals that are merely making a courtesy call by our garden before they head over to some region of the town that will end with them and us on the town Facebook page, again, or a police scanner, again, likely both. Hijinks ensue.

But mostly, I don't tell it those ways, because I am a fountain of rage. I am fury herself. Here is another day when I am torn between vocations, when I am leaping terrified through pricking branches over unruly ground, the bucket of feed too heavy for me. I am wearing the one shirt I'd had left without those Virginia stickseeds on it, and it is catching, yes, has just caught there, on that whole lacework strand of sticking seeds, transferred and stuck, and now I have no more T-shirts. I want to cast them all—animals and people—out of this Eden, and live here "alone in the bee-loud glade."

Sometimes it's even worse, and I worry that I'm not even working like I think I am. What if, after all, I am like Jason in *The Sound and the Fury*, always thinking that I am busy at work, fulfilling my obligations, but I am actually just playing the numbers with other people's money and time, idle and lying, moping my way through a terrible summer? I get through the day and it's hard to narrate what even happened.

Sweating and lost trying to mark out the next pasture, I can't see the forest for the honeysuckle.

"Damn that honeysuckle," writes Faulkner in *The Sound and the Fury*.

Maybe only snippets of fragments and quotations are left to me—no time to put them together: like *The Waste Land*, "What shall we do tomorrow? / What shall we ever do?"

I am a forest full of honeysuckle. What shall I do?

In 1922, after World War I and the Spanish flu epidemic, not many people needed an experimental poem to tell them that Western civilization was a wasteland. No wonder T. S. Eliot asserted, later, a sort of scorn at such a reading: "Some of the more approving critics said that I had expressed the disillusionment of a generation, which is nonsense. I may have expressed for them their own illusion of being disillusioned," but "to me it was only the relief of a personal and wholly insignificant grouse against life."

Thus, in my view, the real question in *The Waste Land* is less "What's wrong with things?" than "Where is relief?" Which is to say that I think the key line of the poem is less the one about shoring up fragments and more "What shall we ever do?" To be able to shore fragments against ruin, the classic synecdoche of the poem, is something, of course. But it wasn't a certainty that the fragments would even get written. Helen Gardner's chronology of *The Waste Land*'s composition acknowledges that Eliot was in despair, and that his friend Ezra Pound's biggest contribution was simply encouragement. For Gardner, Eliot was a man "struggling in ill health and overwork to combine two obligations—his sense of his vocation as a poet, and his duty to the unhappy girl he had married, who was dependent on him." Pound's encouragement made it possible for Eliot to draft and finish one of the great poems of the century.

But I keep wondering about the contribution of—what it cost—"the unhappy girl." Gardner tells us that "apart from Pound, the only person who worked on *The Waste Land* was his wife." Gardner says "it says much for her that she applauded as wonderful what Pound queried as a too photographic, that is realistic, presentation of a failed marriage relation."

> "What shall I do now? What shall I do?"
> "I shall rush out as I am, and walk the street
> "With my hair down, so. What shall we do
>   tomorrow?
> "What shall we ever do?"

Hmmm. What "much" does it say for her, Gardner? Surely not simply that Vivienne Eliot could have a poetic sensibility that Eliot prefers over Pound's at this point.

If the poem-Vivienne's lines "What shall we do tomorrow? / What shall we ever do?" are the center of the thing, the question of vocation comes into focus. The poem becomes less a genealogy of wastelands and more an inquiry into possible treatment protocol, a set of experiments in pilgrimage. Shall we "hurry up," because "it's time"? Shall we "hold on tight"? Shall we "expect nothing"? "Walk around in a ring"?

What does Vivienne's approval of Eliot's lines say for her? Perhaps that she was generous enough to permit him to make lines and questions out of her very own life? Perhaps that she sacrificed her fundamental questions, questions found in her own wasteland, to his need to make things? How about that her words define in this poem the question of his own vocation and hers?

Don't tell me, Gardner, that you haven't thought of the Eliot-Casaubon connection! If Eliot wasn't after the key to all mythologies, then what's a Grail quest for?

Shoring fragments, then, is in this case a prescription. To "give," to "sympathize," to "control," then, are poetic means to this end, but not the only ones offered by the poem. One could "hold on tight" to one's hair-down hair in the street, scrape one's bow across it, fiddle "whisper music." A kind of blues, perhaps.

Here in the forest, it's not lost on me that I live in a land laid waste.

I keep lopping honeysuckle for hours a day, plant myself in the forest, tangle in the nets I'm trying to shape into frames. My wrist, then my elbow, then my ribs burn. I can't grasp things very well.

That rooster died a few weeks after I heard him calling in the afternoon. Inexplicably keeled over in front of the barn he ruled so fiercely: a time to be born, a time to die—no one knows why. Beckett came home from school and dug his grave, out of respect, saving him from the dumpster. Poor child has never even dug in the garden, but he respects the dead. He was like that with Grandma Kriner too—returning to the casket again and again to pat her hand, her cheek, to comfort her, to try and hold her.

The remains of Lily Novak Hansen, who grew up on the farm in the 1940s and '50s, were recently scattered here—and now await resurrection. Her snapshots of the place cataloging the changes are fragments shoring up the soil, clutching the roots. The fake skeleton we'd found in the woods that first day has not yet sprouted, that I see. It disappeared.

On one Wednesday morning, I heard the loud, long, pressing swell of the emergency alert siren test. When it finally died away, then rose the construction sounds, which always begin, it seems, with the resonant repetitive notes of something trying to get through.

⟵

It's just so beautiful, the Lord's best vision of the made-new world, the most just way, the giving tree. In Isaiah,

> They will be called oaks of righteousness,
> the planting of the LORD, to display
>   his glory.
> They shall build up the ancient ruins,
> they shall raise up the former devastations;
> they shall repair the ruined cities,
> the devastation of many generations.

I could see it. I mean, I want to see it—possibly to be it.

It is said in the Talmud that Isaiah was martyred from within a cedar tree—sawn in half, his God-sung tongue. Not a pleasant image, but Isaiah knew, after all, what happens to stumps. The slice of his burnt lips for grafting, his body planted for a shoot.

I think you could read it as happening, Isaiah's vision, at least in part. By the time you get to Mark the Evangelist, Jesus "took the blind man by the hand and led him out of the village, and when he had put saliva on his eyes and laid his hands on him, he asked him, 'Can you see anything?' And the man looked up and said, 'I can see people, but they look like trees, walking.'"

In Zora Neale Hurston's *Their Eyes Were Watching God*, Janie sees her life as a tree, dawn and doom branching out from her. Her whole life moves tree-wise: the efflorescence under the pear tree; her husband, Jody, like the Nebuchadnezzar tree cut down in his pride (always saying, "I god amighty!"); the great hurricane with the one man clinging to a cypress. And she comes home from the quest with the fruit of experience—if not the pears from the bee to her blossom, then the grapefruits the men thought of when they saw her hip pockets.

Always Janie, her arms like branches thrown up to God, asking questions.

Almost all the leaves have been drawn down to the ground now that it is fall. And in the middle of the night from the bathroom window I can see again my favorite branching tree, its supplicatory *v*'s backed by dark. One afternoon, we brought the sheep out of the woods to their winter pasture, a parade led by the organic dog food shaker tambourine.

That last warm day was so rich and rare-lit, church windowed and gleaming. Why so downcast? All along the way was the tangle of branches I'd cut this season—just as overtakeless as the wickets of the living. I thought about this year's things done and undone, what lurks and what might at any moment come crashing down.

Then I saw a flash of wine-dark red close to the ground. I hadn't had much hope of the perseverance of the oaks in the dark of the woods, but here it was, a four-leaf oak sapling, just shy of a foot, making its brave way through the surrounding walnuts.

Oaks drop leaves later than most of the other trees, so now, with most other leaves gone, I could see the oaks: sparse, scattered, as is the way of it for oaks, but still there, and in all four directions. Young snappers, a two-footer by the turn off to the Hidden Five, and in the woods closer to the house, a young adolescent, bent slightly and then straightening up, its leaves red-brown and not faded, saturated with color, poised easterly on their edges thrust from the petiole, as if in wind.

And I went in deeper toward the three-season pond, which was presently dryish. In the wet seasons, the pond has been slowly killing off some massive walnut trees in its midst. It had been a walnut tree there that had nearly fallen on us that day, for example. But at the north side, among the walnuts, lindens, and slippery elm, were two scanty but tall oaks only ten paces apart.

The oaks were thin with the dark and competition, but they stood out because of their proximity to each other. I looked up; they were still scantly leaved, but I saw between them the trunk of a tree—perfectly horizontal—bridging the distance. Eight, maybe ten, inches in diameter, some fifteen or more feet across, the giant tree-section must have broken off one of the dying walnuts nearby and been caught by the oaks. It was now uniquely held there, between the two. As the wind rose, it swayed back and forth, rockabye baby.

Josh has begun to feel better lately. He works a full day, makes dinner, brings chocolate. We go for a walk sometimes in the woods and then turn off on the deer path and cross over to the fields to see the sheep. The wind picks up on the open land, and the bare, tan, dormant grass of the Hidden Five satisfactorily bows to its gusty strength.

When the pasture is in view, we call to Immortal Diamond; she calls back. And when we reach the flock, they greet us. Their thick winter coats are not insensible to a hearty scratch. They are not displeased with such attentions as we give, each called by name. They are pregnant, we can tell now, their sides swelling and moving. Every day we check to see if their bags have ballooned with milk—and guess when the first lamb will come.

Walking back in the forest in the waning day, we see clumps of new-fallen snowflakes. The white of the tail of a deer just there is distinct from the white of the snow in the forest. They, too, bear each the other up.

We talk about the work of the next year. We will replant the Hidden Five. We will drag out the honeysuckle we'd cut. We will plant the acorns we find. Maybe we will make a trail.

He has seen the tiny oak too, he says.

Planted in this forest, we carry her crown.

4

Clearing

We don't love anything unless it's beautiful, do we? . . . What is it that draws us and endears us to the things we love? Unless there were some seemliness and attractiveness in them, there would be no way they could pull us toward themselves.

—Augustine, *Confessions*

*For he grew up before him like a young plant,
and like a root out of dry ground;
he had no form or majesty that we should look at him,
and no beauty that we should desire him.*

—Isaiah 53:2 ESV

Permitted to inhabit neither the realm of the ideal nor the realm of the real, to be neither aspiration nor companion, beauty comes to us like a fugitive bird, unable to fly, unable to land.

—Elaine Scarry, *On Beauty and Being Just*

Owls thrive in these fragmented landscapes humans create.

—*Peterson Reference Guide to Owls
of North America and the Caribbean*

One gray morning this year, the day before my forty-first birthday, I stayed three hours in the rainy woods with an injured, young great horned owl. On the way back to visit the goats in their woodland pasture, nine-year-old Beckett and his friend Gregory had found a big owl in the scrubby grass of the clearing where the paths cross. The owl was failing to fly, flapping into a sort of hop and wing whip, as if to ascend. Then, mission aborted. Something was wrong; the owl was on the ground.

I'd been folding laundry, grounded myself by a not-insignificant funk. Just the night before, a writing collaborator had decided to leave the project we were working on. A total bummer, since we'd both invested more than a year in working together. Was our work not compelling enough to merit the time? Should I even continue with it? What with the birthday coming and all, it seemed appropriate, if somewhat dramatic, to work up the disappointment into a crisis of sorts, modest but ugly.

"You're going to want to come out here," my husband, Josh, said from my lit phone, his voice rustling against the brush in the goat pasture. A giant, messed-up bird, come down to the understory of our wrecked, wet woods. I dropped the dish towels and went to see.

2

For the philosopher Plotinus, beauty exists in the world of forms, away from the corruption of matter. His is an objective view of beauty: things are beautiful to the extent that they conform to the ideal and pattern. I don't agree with Plotinus very much on beauty, but he describes ugliness pretty well: "Suppose a soul to be ugly, ill-disciplined and unjust, full of cravings and all kinds of disturbance, in the midst of fears because of cowardice, and of jealousies because of petty-mindedness, thinking of everything in so far as it thinks of them at all, as mortal and lowly, twisted in every respect, in love with pleasures that are impure." I could resonate.

And while the beauty and ugliness of owl souls are beyond my purview, I'm not so sure that Plotinus wouldn't have declared that owl—at least in its state that day—ugly too. Of course not so psychologically as me. But he does say that whatever is "not mastered by shape and reason principle, since its matter is not capable of supporting complete shaping by the form, is also ugly." The owl was injured, not what he was supposed to be, and in danger, one supposes, of never becoming what he ought to be. That, for Plotinus, is ugly.

The ugliness of both situations was regrettable. But the plain fact is, we would have never stood together on the same ground, that owl and I, if we weren't both of us messed up. He was supposed to be roosting; I was supposed to be working. I don't know what to make of it.

3

We all know what owls mean—by sounds, by images. The *Peterson Reference Guide to Owls of North America and the Caribbean* acknowledges that great horned owls are everyone's mental archetype of owl. They are a classic harbinger of Halloween danger, as those gargantuan neon eyes on the porch at a house downtown remind us.

Or they are brainy knowledge, wisdom. Surely we've seen owls as the theme for a baby's nursery, expressing in hats and adorable onesies the hopes for future intellectual achievement. Or does anyone remember the classic 1970 commercial in which an inquisitive boy consults Mr. Owl to find out how many licks it takes to get to the Tootsie Roll center of a Tootsie Pop?

Once, on each women's bathroom stall of the local high school where we attended a fold-up church, images of owls manifested in a riddle of that commodious literary journal the *Tinkle Times*—no lie—left all summer at eye height: "What asks, but never answers?" Here I presume the owl signifies the angst of a youth population plagued by unending standardized tests. If you, dear student, answer correctly—and by all of your future's hopes, you should at least try to answer the quiz questions, if possible, correctly—then you can see Ms. So-and-So for two tickets to the game.

I never saw Ms. So-and-So, and I hadn't seen actual owls either, great horned or otherwise. Owls had been merely a heap of accepted images to us; recognizable, if tired, symbols. Harry Potter's Hedwig merges them all—a reliable messenger, but usually a bad sign.

4

I walked down the half-grass path through the walnut and oak forest thick with invasive undergrowth. The ground unsteadies at the crossing, what with raspberry, scrub, and the tall-grassed moguls from the former dirt track. It's far from the fruited plain planned by C. C. Miller to support his bee population, and farther still from the oak savanna that preceded him and other white settler immigrants to the town. But the owl had come there: "Owls thrive in these fragmented landscapes humans create," says the *Peterson Reference Guide*.

The clearing seemed crowded. Children in wet sneakers pranced about; Josh, geared up in full flannel and mosquito netting to lay fence for silvopasture, brandished his metal-bladed bushwhacking trimmer; gray catbirds with handsome black caps and fringes swooped down toward the owl, bravely and stupidly. Their distress calls made a soundtrack for the general melee.

Of the owl, my first impression was of a cat—that size—but a mechanical cat, head pivoting round and back at stops on the compass, face toward all of the threats. He did not seem, from my unpracticed eye, to be thriving. His head pivoted again and again, as if looking would tell him what next action might suffice to save him.

He didn't make a sound.

§

Maybe we're just making the owl mean what we've heard owls mean, or maybe we're making him mean what we're feeling at the moment. There's this revenge play by Jo-anna Baillie, *De Monfort*, where just that happens with an owl. In the tensest scene, De Monfort, the eponymous murderer on the hunt for Rezenvelt, hears an owl's cry as a foreshadowing of coming violence: "Foul bird of the night! What spirit guides thee here? / Art thou instinc-tive drawn to scenes of [horror]? / I've heard of this."

But Rezenvelt, De Monfort's blithely unconcerned target, hears in the owl's cry a totally different meaning: his own childhood union with nature. He remembers hooting to the owls "till to my call / He answer would return, and thro' the gloom / We friendly converse held." The thing is, though, De Monfort himself makes the scene of horror—by killing Rezenvelt. He insists on his meaning of the owl, makes it accurate.

Rezenvelt is just as insistent, though. They both die in their certainty of what it means.

That's terrifying, I suppose. But their interpretation of the owl is not the owl, is it?

6

Josh told me he heard an owl while feeding pigs in the woods, a hoot in the predawn dark before market. Josh thought of his dream of raising chickens. The ducks had been all right, mostly—only a few had been taken by foxes, hawks. But chickens seemed more vulnerable—like, well, sitting ducks. A bad sign.

7

Wordsworth's lyric "There Was a Boy," which remembers the poet's experiences with owls in the wilds over Lake Windermere, orbits *De Monfort*—as if he were an audience member of that play trying to figure out the owl. At first, the boy is like Rezenvelt, sharing jovial conversation with owls. He "blew mimic hootings to the silent owls / That they might answer him." The owls would, "responsive to his call," hoot back in "concourse wild / Of jocund din!" So blithe, so halcyon—nature and human in relation.

But then, the bird's meaning changes. The owls refuse to answer the boy. Perhaps the jig is up; he is, after all, not an owl. Perhaps owls are better suited to silence than speech. And in the poem, the owls begin to point through their silent selves not to the boy, or to human concourse with birds, but to the whole of the vale, nature as it reveals transcendent truth. And "in that silence, while he hung / Listening," the visible scene

> Would enter unawares into his mind
> With all its solemn imagery, its rocks,
> Its woods, and that uncertain heaven
> received
> Into the bosom of the steady lake.

Silenced by the silent owls, the boy can see the world outside his own purposes or speech.

Then the owls change again. Whatever this nature is, it's not just picturesque, or even the gentle sublime Wordsworth imagined for children: "This boy was taken from his mates, and died / In childhood, ere he was full twelve years old." The birds come back around to forewarning death.

But "There Was a Boy" doesn't end with the death of the boy. Immediately after the lines about his death, Wordsworth continues, "Preeminent in beauty is the vale / Where he was born and bred." The owls come eventually to take their place, silently, to mean something like beauty.

Hard to think how beauty could work like that, so near this boy's death—that it's in fact seen by Wordsworth only because of the silence pervading the churchyard and his own silence. "A long half-hour together I have stood," he writes, "Mute—looking at the grave in which he lies!"

But even simple, profound beauty isn't the final meaning of Wordsworth's owls. "There Was a Boy" was written in 1799 and published in the second edition of *The Lyrical Ballads*. But it was later placed into the bosom of *The Prelude* in 1805—a poem about the growth of the poet's mind, which work itself was prefatory to his great, unfinished poem, *The Recluse*. The planned work, *The Recluse*, would demonstrate how the mind, "when wedded to this goodly universe / In love and holy passion," can renew the common world. Its mission was to sing

> Of Truth, of Grandeur, Beauty, Love,
> and Hope,
> And melancholy Fear subdued by Faith;
> Of blessed consolations in distress;
> Of moral strength, and intellectual Power;
> Of joy in widest commonalty spread;
> Of the individual Mind that keeps her own
> Inviolate retirement, subject there
> To Conscience only, and the law supreme
> Of that Intelligence which governs all—

If successful, the work would cheer "Mankind in times to come."

Setting those owls, that alive and dead boy, in book 5 of *The Prelude* changes their meaning. It makes them a way to think about how experiences of nature's beauty are preparation for the poet's vocation, a correction to the mind merely attendant on bookish fantasy. The owls become a way to teach the world about the wonder, the mystery, of beauty.

And the manuscript history of those key lines shows how much wondering, how little certainty, goes into beauty. In 1799, they went, "Preeminent in beauty is the vale / Where he was born and bred." In 1805, he tried, "Fair are the woods and beauteous is the spot, / The vale where he was born." In 1850, when the final manuscript of *The Prelude* was published posthumously, it came out that he had tried again: "Fair is the spot, most beautiful the vale / Where he was born."

Hard to think how beauty could be part of our own losses, our own failures at speaking, our own vocational sloughs and stops. What to do? At the end of *The Prelude*, the poet rises "as if on wings," looking over all the world he's been "centring all in love." His conclusion? "In the end / All gratulant if rightly understood."

Die trying.

8

"Death is the mother of beauty," wrote Wallace Stevens in his repudiation-of-Christianity poem, "Sunday Morning," "hence from her, / Alone, shall come fulfilment to our dreams / And our desires."

Death giving birth to beauty. That idea seemed so horrible to me. I've worried over this poem with students for years. It is, I say, among the most beautiful poems I've ever read—second maybe to "That Nature Is a Heraclitean Fire and of the Comfort of the Resurrection" by Gerard Manley Hopkins. Stevens's descriptions of "moods in falling snow" and "gusty / Emotions on wet roads on autumn nights" seemed indeed "measures destined for [*my*] soul" too, not just the soul of the woman in the poem.

It was the war, perhaps—Stevens having to deal with "the heavenly fellowship of men that perish," reminding all that death is coming. He's making the point, maybe, that death makes desire endure, makes all the beautiful meanings. "The consummation of the swallow's wings" is desire's flight, not its finish. The elongated arc of the wing is itself concentrated longing.

Even Stevens had to take another go, though—and in the same poem. He repeats the phrase in another take: "Death is the mother of beauty, mystical, / Within whose burning bosom we devise / Our earthly mothers waiting, sleeplessly." The meaning of "death" expands with additional referents.

Stevens was trying, in poems, to show the mind finding what would suffice—if not Christ. In "Of Modern Poetry," he says, "It must / Be the finding of a satisfaction, and may / Be of a man skating, a woman dancing, a woman / Combing. The poem of the act of the mind."

There's this story in Juliet Barker's biography of Wordsworth. As an old man skating, "one hand tucked into his shirt front, the other into his waist band," he tripped on a stone. Barker writes, "Despite the assault on his dignity, he had the good grace to accept the accident cheerfully, merely sitting up and remarking to a watching child, 'Eh boy, that was a bad fall, wasn't it?'" Beautiful old man Wordsworth and that boy; beautiful that fall, and even the landing crash. Barker says he "starred the ice" with his fall.

In that same Wallace Stevens poem, the last lines are: "At evening, casual flocks of pigeons make / Ambiguous undulations as they sink / Downward to darkness, on extended wings."

There's a debate that pops up every once in a while in Wallace Stevens studies: was his reported deathbed conversion to Christianity real? Who gets to say?

9

Who can even see these days? Here's what I mourn in my owl story: my idol phone.

In *On Beauty and Being Just*, Elaine Scarry writes that "out of the requirement beauty places on us to replicate, the simplest manifestation . . . is the everyday fact of staring. The first flash of the bird incites the desire to duplicate not by translating the glimpsed image into a drawing or a poem or a photograph but simply by continuing to see her five seconds, twenty-five seconds, forty-five seconds later—as long as the bird is there to be beheld." For me, the photograph of the owl came first, the staring second.

I posted the owl on social media immediately, justifying myself with the thought that maybe someone would send advice: "Injured owl at Root and Sky Farm! Don't know how to help!" I scoured the internet to find what kind of owl he was because adolescents don't look the same as adults. I looked up what to do when an owl crosses your path—besides, say, throwing salt over your left shoulder to ward off danger.

I texted my biologist-forester friend, but she was in Wyoming sampling rivers with students. I texted the provost of our college—she was, coincidentally, also in Wyoming with the students. They sent cheerful pictures of the young people wading through sunny patches of river water.

Eventually, I got a message to a woman at the rescue center. The animal control officer was busy and couldn't come, but she could come herself—if I could wait a few hours. And so I settled in—grabbing a cup of coffee, some sunflower seeds, an apple, and the umbrella, for a steady rain had begun—for a wait.

My phone's battery was draining. I guess it was going to take itself out of the story anyway. All idols are false, by definition.

I kept telling myself, *Look at the owl. You never get an opportunity like this.* "Little we see the nature that is ours," Wordsworth chided me, in my mind. Here was—no, maybe not the sea, baring her bosom to the moon, but an owl, secret as the night woods itself, baring his breast to me, though of course, unwillingly. And I was looking with my phone instead of my eyes.

My lens couldn't get the droplets of water on him—how they silvered his feathers to a shine spark. It couldn't get how, when I looked up into the sky at a floating hawk, the owl looked up at the hawk too—both of us at the day-shift raptor brother-enemy. His pupils narrowed at the white of the sky, and when we both looked down again—at each other again—his eyes were almost completely pencil-yellow. Or was it gym-floor yellow? Or legal-pad yellow?

"Staring," and now we're back to Elaine Scarry again, "is a version of the wish to create."

10

On February 24, 1915, the English poet Edward Thomas wrote a poem called "The Owl." Thomas had been working as a literary journalist, grinding out gristmill reviews for measly cash. He often worked from 9 a.m. to 1 a.m., breaking only for chores and homeschooling duties. His reviews made careers for others, including Robert Frost.

The last three years of Thomas's life, when he was pressed down by war, depression, and vocational troubles, poetry finally spilled over from him. In 1917, the year of his death at age thirty-nine by a shell blast through the chest at the Battle of Arras, his book came out.

My copy of Thomas's poems came to me from the poet Brett Foster, for years my next-door office neighbor. Brett's best poems, a bit like Thomas's, poured out in a blaze of sick beauty at the end of his life. Brett was shot through the gut too, but with cancer.

Brett had bought the Thomas book used; it had been owned by a respectable Keats scholar before him. When Brett died, his wife, Anise, opened his office and let us take volumes that were important to us. I took back *Robert's Rules of Order*, which I'd bought for him on his fortieth birthday as a joke commemorating those early years when we wondered whether our own books would be lost in a sea of institutional negotiations. I also took the Thomas, a slim, jacketed hardcover, without knowing why. I didn't open it for two years after he died. When I did, I saw that Brett had made a single hatch mark by several poems that meant something to him. "The Owl," though, had two marks.

When the bird became flesh among us, as it were, I took up the volume and read. "The Owl" tells a simple story of a journeying poet coming in from cold, weary hunger to an inn for warmth, rest, and dinner. It's all a lovely satisfaction, except that an owl's cry reminds him of the true gorgeousness of the comfort he has received, and the terrible sadness that others don't get it.

Clearing

Downhill I came, hungry, and yet not
        starved;
Cold, yet had heat within me that was proof
Against the North wind; tired, yet so
        that rest
Had seemed the sweetest thing under a roof.
Then at the inn I had food, fire, and rest,
Knowing how hungry, cold, and tired was I.
All of the night was quite barred out except
An owl's cry, a most melancholy cry
Shaken out long and clear upon the hill,
No merry note, nor cause of merriment,
But one telling me plain what I escaped
And others could not, that night, as in
        I went.
And salted was my food, and my repose,
Salted and sobered, too, by the bird's voice
Speaking for all who lay under the stars,
Soldiers and poor, unable to rejoice.

This poem is not a moral lesson in how to get outside ourselves, not exactly. Rather, it's an avian *ars poetica*, a way to consider the relationship between a messed-up self and a warring world. It is more than anything a way to consider whatever might be said or made of any of it—"what to make of a diminished thing," as Thomas's friend Robert Frost would put it in "The Oven Bird."

The reader can tell something's wrong with the speaker by the inverted syntax that dogs the lines. To make the words fit—and remember with Plotinus that the beautiful must be mastered by pattern—all must be torqued upward toward the resolving rhyme. There it is in "Downhill I came," "Hungry, cold, and tired was I," and "in I went."

Whatever the internal chaos was, the poem tries to insist, it might be managed. All those "yet," "yet," "yets" try. It's how we might tell friends—the ones we don't want to bother—the story of some slough of despondency. It was bad, yes, but not that bad. Look, the downhill way could be seen as the relief of the end of the journey, not only as a sinking slide, right?

Not so fast. The rumpled rhythm—trochees for line openings, interjections, and such—cries no such thing. Thomas may have been trying to avoid the facilities of conventional poetry by borrowing prose rhythms—he wrote in a letter as much. But he tries to hold up the standards of form too. That will rather scatter a person.

And the biggest disturbance in the poem is the titular call itself—"An owl's cry, a most melancholy cry." The owl's call lurches Thomas—himself and his lines—away from a romantic conversation between nature and self, away even from the impress of beauty on the self that undoes you. It calls back to the salted sadness of the open sky and the open eye—to no personal bliss of daffodils, nor repose, only need, the night road.

By poem's end, all the desperate non-pattern-keepers rock the lines. The last three lines start with trochees, not iambs, as the salt of the earth comes in to lines and minds, stressed as they are.

Thomas followed his own poetry to the war. "Now all roads lead to France," he wrote; it was the road to be taken. "Unable to rejoice" sounds about right.

//

Therefore I will wail and howl, I will go stripped and naked: I will make a wailing like the dragons, and mourning as the owls.

—Micah 1:8 KJV

We used to give each other Micah 1:8, one of the few biblical references to owls, at summer camp. We'd get special Jesusy Post-its from the Christian Supply store and write the reference to that verse on it. We'd slip it into someone's hands, saying, "I just feel like the Lord laid this verse on my heart for you." And snicker. Anything with nakedness, you understand.

We had good intentions; we'd look up the verses in devotions. But we thought the key verse of Micah was SIX eight, not ONE eight—about the Lord's requirements.

Sing it with me: but to do justly (but to do justly) . . .

Those minor prophets knew us better than we knew ourselves. I read them all one summer afternoon on a day trip from camp to what we called Moshier Falls, a natural rock waterslide where we could picnic and slide all day. It was the final bit of my first read-through of the whole Bible—all those short books poured into me in a great gush. How closely they link, those prophets—Habakkuk, Micah, all of them—the gorgeous beauty of the Lord God's saving power and the disgusting ugliness of human injustice. "Look! The LORD is coming from his dwelling place!" says Micah. "His splendor was like the sunrise; rays flashed from his hand," says Habakkuk. Here comes beauty—not just in spite of but *because of* the worst. He comes to us, messed up. Wish we could have seen that.

12

His head was a fuzzed, dun softball, rain furred. Small, tufty ridges highlighted the forthcoming brows. The widow's peak descended severely to the beak in would-be angry eyebrows of white, if it weren't for the equal and opposite force—curved letter *c*'s, sweeping skates of brown up the outside of his eyes, suggesting questions.

His eye marbles were lensed with a clear glass thickness. Under the crystal knob, they were, I felt, the precise yellow of a #2 Dixon Ticonderoga pencil. Dilating pupils, feather-ringed by interrupted circles smudging gray and brown and orange—a weighted gaze. His eyes amassed orbiters like twin suns.

My massive inertia lurched. There was gravity there. I tripped my way slowly over the mini-moraines of the clearing. I thought to project myself as a nonplanet—Pluto, even—a rock chip, drawing toward this grounded sun of a bird in slow, deliberate, narrowing circles. Ten feet. Six feet. Five feet, and, finally, four feet away. I was this close in the gray morning, only the length of my useless desk between me and one of the great raptors of the night woods.

His aspect was all intention—no, not intention; *attention*. Only the violet underlid occasionally slow-closed in what Josh called a mascara blink (the violet did have an eyeshadow look to it) against the gold and gray and brown. I could see the lighted underfeathers. A harlequin, or harlot, tipping buff-gold petticoats; he was jacketed in cascades of variegated feathers, trimmed in undulating sandbars of white, buff, tan, sienna. I could see all the layers of softness required to remain silent in flight, and at night. One wing in disarray.

His head turning was like a royal's, dispensing attention; all his finery was that of a hunter-king, girded up, girthed about, with worthy furs.

13

> The fact that something is perceived as beautiful is bound up with an urge to protect it, or act on its behalf.
> —Elaine Scarry, *On Beauty and Being Just*

> The Spirit of the Sovereign LORD is on me,
> because the LORD has anointed me
> . . . .
> to comfort all who mourn,

and provide for those who grieve in Zion—
to bestow on them a crown of beauty
instead of ashes . . .
                                                    —Isaiah 61:1–3 NIV

Is every birdcall vocational? Karl Barth would call the owl, being creation, beneficial, covenantal. Before seeing that owl, we might have been said to be the sort who would consent cheerfully to admire the owl's glories, if it were convenient. Had we thought about it, we would have wished to be on the right side of owl protection against herbicides, should taking sides be called for. Our social media likes and shares would not have failed to speak out.

In the owl's presence, though, I wanted to save him. And I feared that if I left him, even for a few minutes, he would hop away to hide somewhere in the bent undergrowth and die. But it was by no means certain that my presence was salvific in any way. What did I know of owls? I got too close, two feet away—and learned that great horned owls hiss, just like cats, just like your skin when it touches the pan. And then, when the rain picked up, I unthinkingly raised my golf umbrella, and that owl puffed out his feathers so far he enlarged himself by half— in what I supposed was fright prompted by my peacocky fantail of o'erweening might. He tried again to fly away but got only a few feet. I had hurt and frightened him.

He paused again, waiting, looking at me without pause, and in a half hour, when the rain had more or less soaked him through, he walked into a dense honeysuckle thicket and stood, drier, under the hedge. Still never ceasing to look.

I followed in a panic, tripping over the moguls, frantic as a chicken. I dashed the empty coffee mug back into the soaked grass, chucked the apple core somewhere, tucked the empty bag of sunflower kernels into my pocket. And I stepped forward, back, up, down, trying to find the right angle, in the rain, through the branches, past the catbirds all gray and black and fine that circled him, unceasingly sentinel. I found the owl still looking at me without moving. So I looked as hard as I could, into the dim, to the dark center of those owl's eyes. I stood in the steady rain under the darkest of umbrellas, grass water dampening up my jeans, trying to stay still. Trying to look. Trying not to look at my dying phone.

I thought, stand and wait, stand and wait. "They also serve who only stand and wait." If I could just stay with the owl so that he didn't get lost, he had a chance of getting rescued by people who could help.

"I will climb up to my watchtower and stand at my guard post."

But then I glanced to the left as gushing-down rain hit the goat-stripped raspberry canes, dropping on the immature Queen Anne's lace and the many purple faces of heal-all.

No, look at the owl. Where were his eyes again? There. I didn't want to lose him.

For the last forty minutes or so, phone battery dead, it was just me and the rain and the owl, catbirds circling around. His gaze never wavered. It took me the whole time to give up, settle down, and look back.

Thirteen licks is not enough to look to an owl.

He was fine, he was beautiful, even if he was messed up. He was beautiful—as theologian Alejandro García-Rivera writes in *The Community of the Beautiful*—as "what moves the heart" is beautiful.

14

And this contemplation of mine burbled up in my mind from the inmost recesses of my heart, and I wrote some volumes entitled "On the Beautiful and the Fitting." I think two or three of them—you know, God, but I forget. We haven't got them anymore; they've wandered away from us somehow.

—Augustine, *Confessions*

When the rescuer came—her name was Dawn—she crouched into the brush with her falconer's gloves and grasped his legs, inverting him, achieving instant calm.

She brought him out into the clearing to examine the wing. Her hands were confident as they slid over his wings to determine the injury. I peered at his massive talons, vestiges of a dinosaur past.

"Look," she said, "here." I saw feathers worn off against a slim bone, a scrape of blood. "And yes," she said, "here it is, a break in the proximal ulna."

She looked at me. "You stayed out here with him the whole time?"

"Yep."

"That's nice of you," she said.

She told us they had a mother at the center who'd take care of him. They'd set the wing, give him something for the pain. She put him into a box like one of those coffee carriers from Tim Hortons and set it on the front seat. He was perfectly quiet and still.

"Sorry about the state of my car," she said. "You can fill out the form on the clipboard there."

The form had a box to check if we wanted to receive an email about the animal's "final disposition." (A parenthetical note here requested a minimum fifty-dollar donation if so.) I waited until October to ask for my email, for his final disposition.

I said I'd been writing about the owl, trying to figure him out. "Thank you for contacting us!" came the reply. "We will respond to your message as quickly as possible!"

Since then, one Facebook friend, who lives in Utah now, posted a photo of the owl she found on the hood of her car—it made her late to her mammogram.

Another friend, from down the road, showed me a photo of an owl on the roof of her chicken coop, covered in chicken guts and gore, eye bloody and feathers ruffled from the death match.

At daybreak recently, my husband was moving the cows in the pasture and saw another great horned owl float from the finger jut of forest to the treed field's edge.

But about this owl, we've received no message, yet.

And let the beauty of the LORD our God be upon us:
and establish thou the work of our hands upon us;
yea, the work of our hands establish thou it.

—Psalm 90:17 KJV

5

Wattle

It is true that all this moral significance is contained in the word "holy," but it includes in addition—as even we cannot but feel—a clear overplus of meaning, and this it is now our task to isolate.

—Rudolf Otto, *The Idea of the Holy*

*H*allowed be—how, no one can come into the bramble of this forest—honeysuckle and multi-flora rose, bindweed and gooseberry, creeping Charlie and garlic mustard—

Hallowed be—how, supposed to be that Minnesota was his way in to a new start—to bounce out of the out-of-bounds was, in effect, to stay in line on the good side—how, but he got laid off when they all had COVID.

Hallowed be—how, that word "asylum" might not mean that.

Spring is the mischief in me and I wonder
If I could put a notion in his head:
                    —Robert Frost, "Mending Wall"

Hallowed be—how, but something slithered into their lungs' hollows, coils of thorny, serpentine something—

Hallowed be—how, it was hard to know what it was, with no clear definition, no tests in the Midwest—

There is only one way to help another to an understand-
ing of it. He must be guided and led on by consideration

and discussion of the matter through the ways of his own
mind, until he reach the point at which the numinous in
him perforce begins to stir, to start into life and into con-
sciousness. We can co-operate in this process.
　　　　　　　　　　　—Rudolf Otto, *The Idea of the Holy*

Hallowed be—how, the unflagging advance of the thicket up the hill of the yard—how, ash-leaf maple and basswood and black walnut and fleabane and ragweed—how, the neighbor said it was so clear just seven years ago—

Hallowed be—how, the psychologist showed me the scores and said, "Well, you don't have ADHD"—how, but, I'm not sure I've had a clear thought in months, let alone a clear sentence.

Just get people thinking. About what a fence can or
cannot do.
　　　　　　　—Viewer comment on Ai Weiwei's NYC community
　　　　　　　　　art project, *Good Fences Make Good Neighbors*

Hallowed be—how, if I could just get some space to think about it!

Hallowed be—how, maybe if I put a wattle fence here, the ducks will stay out and I can have one ordered, tidy space with some flowers, where it at least looks neat.

Hallowed be—how, at evening chores, the fog in the pasture was white enough that it seemed to delay rather than hasten the night's coming on—how, the field felt like a snow globe in reverse, the snow outside, and I was in the bubble, it moving with me—how, one feels in fog, preserved, bewildered, the tiny insulate globe itself a wide eye, surrounded by whiteness around—how, just branches and dead grass and the white of the edges of everything—

Why is light given to one who cannot see the way, whom
God has fenced in?

—Job 3:23

Hallowed be—how, frequently asked questions order askers, not answers—

Hallowed be—how, he says, "This is what your Christians do," but mostly stays silent.

Hallowed be—how, God, the college bubble used to be a joke!

Hallowed be—how, I guess I wouldn't even know how to ask the question anyway?

He moves in darkness as it seems to me,
Not of woods only and the shade of trees.

—Robert Frost, "Mending Wall"

Hallowed be—how, it all feels dead in these woods—how, still the rope of wild grapevine around the branches—how, white and quiet even the sky, the desolate road.

Hallowed be—how, a cough was just then not enough—
how, it was so dry you couldn't expel anything.

Hallowed be—how, malaise makes its way, tendriling,
choking, poisoning before you know it.

Hallowed be—how, he told him he got shot that way
before another time by police—how, he said, "I just had
COVID, man; I don't want to go back to that."

Hallowed be—how, we call him, the guy with all the
posted No Trespassing, Video Surveillance, and No Soliciting signs, the "scary neighbor"—he has a line of pines
back of his piece—for a natural castling fort against our
acreage—three years and we haven't met him yet—

Hallowed be—how, I know nothing about you lately,
Lord—what I know and do is consume, consume, consume—and of course, zoom.

He says again, 'Good fences make good neighbors.'
—Robert Frost, "Mending Wall"

Hallowed be—how, we hear the scary neighbor's
chainsaw cutting something down all March—how, his
gun shoots what we hope during sleepless nights is not
our sheep or dog or another person or himself—how,
sometimes back there, behind that row of pines, in the
Hidden Five acres, I sing in the poor pasture, find coyotes
slinking off into the forest edge of the field—

Hallowed be—how, the notary came—how, I cleaned
for hours—how, I bleached even our licenses—how,

I hoped she wouldn't accept my offer of coffee just in case we might have something—how, I worried that she couldn't stay home—how, her race did not escape me—how, she said she figured it was all overblown—how, we tried above all not to cough—how, we needed that refinance pretty badly, but that's no excuse—

Hallowed be—how, it's always that way—what if they come before I'm finished tidying, and they always come before I'm finished—they'll know—how, I've never forgiven my mother-in-law for not telling me that one time they were on the way until they were an hour from arriving even though she's forgiven me for far worse—how, but I can tidy until they come—how, right now, tidying—

> *Therefore come out from them, and be separate from them, says the Lord, and touch nothing unclean; then I will welcome you.*
>
> —2 Corinthians 6:17

Hallowed be—how, that notary, she was the last non-family member to come into our home until the Fourth of July.

Hallowed be—how, again the hours have gone—how, I haven't seen you at all—how, sometimes I like it that way.

Hallowed be—how, I sewed the masks wide—how, I ironed them, surrounded them with tiny, tidy white stitches—how, all you can see is eyes and their ambiguous crinkle—

Hallowed be—how, these hopes that we could keep from hurting each other—by cordoning ourselves off from others' very breath in a globe composed of wind.

Hallowed be—how, Julian walled herself into a hollow hazelnut amphitheater—how, she found boundary workable for trying to say.

Hallowed be—how, it didn't probably keep out the plague or, honestly, even let her escape—how, everyone knew where she was if they wanted her—and I guess they did want her—

> *. . . for you yourself warned us, saying, "Set limits around*
> *the mountain and keep it holy."*
>
> —Exodus 19:23

Hallowed be—how, a chainsaw requires desire so raw it's like anger, the blast of tearing pull—again, again, again—your arm in an action that doesn't accrete, doesn't progress, but must above all concentrate.

Hallowed be—how, it doesn't start the first time, ever. Or the second.

Hallowed be—how, each pull requires the same blast, precision, focus—or greater—that it requires more because starting with the second pull, the muscles begin to tire.

Hallowed be—how, whatever that was in the shoulder rips—how, the anger and sear—how, the swear—of the arm.

Hallowed be—how, the danger, when it kicks up for good, requires Robert Frost's "Out, Out—"—requires

166

a memory of your own death—but in advance, like for Hezekiah or something.

Hallowed be—how, his line "No one believed" that the boy's pulse could dim that quickly after having his hand cut off is instructional—how, your line must be a revision of it—how, it must be in fact "I believe; help my unbelief"—how, that you must believe you will die in short order that you may not die right now.

Hallowed be—how, chainsaws require that you know you will stop when there is a near miss—how, you decide to halt when a large branch you've just sawed down knocks your helmet too hard—how, when you drop the saw, with the safety on, but still—how, when you trip almost, it works an alert that you had wearied more than you knew—how, you see then, again, that you almost died just there.

Hallowed be—how, at every stage you must know when to call it a day—that this is why days, in fact, are—to be called—how, Genesis 1:5 proves it—

Hallowed be—how, the most important thing is to pay very close attention to what you are cutting down, and to what you are building.

> *I placed a jar in Tennessee,*
> *And round it was, upon a hill.*
> *It made the slovenly wilderness*
> *Surround that hill.*
>
> —Wallace Stevens, "Anecdote of the Jar"

Hallowed be—how, the saplings drag and tangle when I pull them up the hill—how, sweat and breath—how, body and heartpound—how, a real body just plods, and even that only if you're white.

Hallowed be—how, but the rod in the fence post pounder is a clapper—how, I lift the heavy pounder bell above my head again and again—nearly beyond my strength—its dip, when I let it down, is the resound.

Hallowed be—how, a portable fence for any given animal means "this is green pasture"—

Hallowed be—how, Ai Weiwei, when he made that show about refugees and fences in New York City, finally just had to acknowledge it—how, "this work really comes out not from creativity but from regulations—like most of my work."

Hallowed be—how, even Yahweh used a portable enclosure—how, they called it the tent of meeting—how, Moses wore a mask out of there to keep from hurting people—how, Joshua wouldn't leave.

Hallowed be—how, you could also call it a frame—how, also a nest, which word occurred to me as I wattled it in, the ducks in their quack racket making their way all around.

> The LORD is my chosen portion and my cup;
> > you hold my lot.
> The boundary lines have fallen for me in pleasant places;
> > I have a goodly heritage.
>
> —Psalm 16:5–6

Hallowed be—how, a portable fence for animals, say, sheep, of course, does not mean freedom, except freedom from hurting the land, from sinking in their own waste—how, of course, that's nothing to be sneezed at.

Hallowed be—how, a finger over the post's rough bark slides like a pianist's—how, like Huntley Brown's—how, it slides *con fuerza*—how, with nothing so simple as ebullience—how, nor ease, though it may look like ease—how, nor grace under pressure—how, nor simply play—how, rather ample—how, his glissandos nerve out, distinct over a whole orchestra—how, when he plays at a funeral—Rodney Sisco's funeral—the resurrection is immanent—

Hallowed be—how, just then I noticed that—the post itself has leafed out—a bunch of them have—rooted down and lifted up—how, the post and the finger withies are making something new after being cut down.

True salvation is a heavy weight, and wholeness is no trifling matter. Authentic salvation moves beyond your individual spiritual and physical health and encompasses all those around you.

—Yolanda Pierce,
In My Grandmother's House:
Black Women, Faith, and the Stories We Inherit

Hallowed be—how, Pastor Tate said on Twitter recently that every breath you take is a victory you take away from the enemy.

Hallowed be—how, the internet has frustrated us so many times that Rhonda rebukes Satan at the beginning of every meeting we have.

Hallowed be—how, they think maybe new laws will help keep them from shooting them—

Hallowed be—how, the Lord is my keeper, the Lord who sings over me—how, the Lord is a mother hen—how, the Lord hems me in behind and before—how, I am afraid of my own sin, that it will hurt others—how, it will make them love me less—

Hallowed be—how, Tamir Rice—how, George Floyd—how, Philando Castile—how, Breonna Taylor—how, Michael Brown—how, Eric Garner—how, Trayvon Martin—

Hallowed be—how, are they just kindling?—how, are we bent into a fence?

> So, the buffered identity of the disciplined individual moves in a constructed social space, where instrumental rationality is a key value, and time is pervasively secular. All of this makes up what I want to call "the immanent frame."
>
> —Charles Taylor, *A Secular Age*

Hallowed be—how, Charlotte told me, in her five-year-old way, that God beeps inside her—how, she said, God is SO big that he can be with everyone at the same time—how, she said, God is real and she can prove it—how, but just then, when I was waiting for her answer with everything in me, she said, "And that's the end of my sentence," and left me alone on the screened-in-porch.

Hallowed be—how, in deaths of migrants in statistics compiled by the US Border Patrol and arranged by fiscal year, "data may change based on new discovery of remains and possible dates determined by a medical examiner."

"Very truly, I tell you, anyone who does not enter the sheepfold by the gate but climbs in by another way is a thief and a bandit."

—John 10:1

Hallowed be—how, the very first time I touched an electric fence, walking the west coast of Ireland—how, I wanted to find some sort of shortcut back, to give up— how, the wire where I touched it when I failed the hurdle blast-stung each striation, agonist/antagonist at once— how, my leg jutted out, an alien other—how, hamstrung, how, wrung, how, the ringing gong of it—how, I learned just then to use profanity—

Hallowed be—how, in the nineteenth-century records of the Illinois State Horticultural Society, Mr. Weir said, of the ash-leaf maple, "It is not a tree we wish to see live"—

Hallowed be—how, but still, I do the same thing— how, I can only feel all right in my fence's tree cutting if I think of them as "invasive species"—

Hallowed be—how, I as a citizen regret that the term "junk tree" is designated as "American" in the OED.

One of the ideas that is expressed again and again by
Native cultures is that their sacred ways are inseparable
from the ordinary. Most evangelical Christians . . . have
compartmentalized worldviews.

—Richard Twiss / Taoyate Obnajin
(He Stands with His People),
One Church, Many Tribes

Hallowed be—how, when our neighbor saw my withies wattled, flowers finally blooming—months after I'd littered the ground he patiently mows for me with twigs that chewed up his mower—how, he said, "You've made your own Eden"—

Hallowed be—how, I was just trying to make some order out of the chaos!

Hallowed be—how, he said if you had a lot of money, what I would do is clear out all of this—how, his bad-shouldered arm swept across the front acres of advancing grove from which I'd drawn the fence wood—here.

As I lay there I felt the earth pulling at my body. It seemed
I could actually feel my gravity, which I pictured some-
how as a huge molten magnet sitting at the center of the
earth. I could feel it drawing on me and draining me of

strength. I was going past limits, boundaries, to where
nothing made sense.

—Louise Erdrich, *The Round House*

Hallowed be—how, soon my flexor carpi ulnaris twinged and burned at every twist of the wrist—at all of the thousands of squeaking ratchet-action trimmer clips—at each grasp of a fence post to waggle and wrench it from the ground, at each strike of the hammer to pound it in again—how, then it was lifting the cast iron pan too, or whisking hot fudge sauce, being jostled—how, I can't even consider going to the doctor or resting it—how, even a brace doesn't keep it from hurting.

Hallowed be—how, the thing about electric fences is that any animal must truly believe in the fence—how, all the magazines say it—how, an animal must respect the fence, or—how, it must be culled immediately—how, it's because it will keep getting out—how, it will be leading the flock or the herd away—how, if they try to escape, it can lead to "tragedy."

Hallowed be—how, "culled" is a euphemism for "killed"—how, it's not a very good one.

Hallowed be—how, that system must assume some overabundance of animals—how, we have like eighteen sheep, what, are we just going to kill them?—how, and but who has access to processors like that?—how, and what processors can drop everything to cull your fence-agnostic animals into, yes, smaller-than-end-of-season-target-sized-yet-still-delicious chops during a time of pandemic?

Hallowed be—how, apparently, we are a seeker-sensitive family farm?

> *"Oh that you would bless me and enlarge my border, and*
> *that your hand might be with me, and that you would*
> *keep me from hurt and harm!"*
>
> —1 Chronicles 4:10

Hallowed be—how, 222 miles of the Trump wall have been constructed along the US-Mexico border, as of this writing—how, the website trumpwall.construction details the sections on a tidy table, with a header that says, "Work in progress, please be gentle"—

Hallowed be—how, the boy in "Out, Out—" was doing the work when his hand did not refuse to shake with the chainsaw—how, even though a child, "He saw all spoiled"—how, you can't keep anything from "spilling," cannot keep the life in him by holding a chainsawed arm up like a jar, like "Take this cup"—how, every time I use the chainsaw I think of him—how, I build on his arm—

Hallowed be—how, your fence must be perfect—how, sheep netting is rarely perfect—how, you must make it perfect—how, you must walk it down again and again if there are branches and weeds—how, if the signal is weak—how, it could be anything or nothing—how, I found the whole flock out that afternoon, down by the barn—

Hallowed be—how, it was Father's Day—how, I'd meant to give Josh a day off from the chores—how, but I had to call him when the sheep were out—

Hallowed be—how, we found the one sheep dead in the tangle—wrestled, twisted, wrenched, dragged down—the whole thing down—how, we had to cut the fence apart in a dozen places to get him out—

Hallowed be—how, his name was Ignatius of Loyola—how, he was born the spring of 2020 in the same cohort as Julian, Thomas Merton, Gustavo Gutiérrez, and James Cone—how, his penultimate Sunday, we had snuggled for photos when I was out on a morning walk—how, I remarked on and knew him by the smallest margin of fawn coloring along the edges of his ears—how, and Josh dug the grave under the big tree—

Hallowed be—how, while Josh dug, I moved all the rest of the fences and pounded them in again amidst the thigh-high clover—how, each strike of the orange hammer hurt my wrecked arm.

Hallowed be—how, I brought the sheep in the fence again.

> *Something there is that doesn't love a wall,*
> *That wants it down.*
>
> —Robert Frost, "Mending Wall"

Hallowed be—how, but are you a good witch or a bad witch?

Hallowed be—how, we actually met the scary neighbor last week—how, because again, the fence didn't keep the sheep in in that forest—how, the man we couldn't meet for three years of Good Friday hot cross buns or mental wishes in a direction, came to the front door to tell us the sheep—but he thought they were goats because of the breed—were out and visiting his yard—

Hallowed be—how, that one sheep, Spot, will follow you anywhere if you have a handful of Louise's grain-free salmon-and-sweet-potato dog food, so it wasn't that big a deal to get them back in—how, plus Immortal Diamond and Johnny are always going to want a scratch—how, and sheep do follow—

Hallowed be—how, Mike, the neighbor, talked to me for a half hour—how, how relieved he was that we weren't going to develop the property—how, that we weren't going to let chemicals leach into the pond—how, he designs massive machines for factories—how, he leaves the town alone and they leave him alone—how, he's been burned before—how, the signs, though, the posted signs—how, they are not for *us*—how, that loaf of bread I gave him was the best he'd tasted in his entire life—

> 'Why do they make good neighbors? Isn't it
> Where there are cows?' But here there are no cows.
> Before I built a wall I'd ask to know
> What I was walling in or walling out,
> And to whom I was like to give offense.
>
> —Robert Frost, "Mending Wall"

Wattle

Hallowed be—how, there is no tension like the tension of needing to get a steer on a trailer when there is a rare, lucky appointment at the processer during a pandemic when you're running low on burgers and especially when the steer in question is Three.

Hallowed be—how, the placement of movable fences in a pasture toward the loading the steer on a trailer requires perfection in set-up, requires the steer to both believe the electric fence and be willing to step up onto a trailer or believe there are no other options—how, we've done it a bunch of times—how, but in a nonpermanent set-up, well, it's not easy—how, the set-up itself can take several hours, to create a funnel of fencing, a chute of precisely the minimum width—

Hallowed be—how, if you fail on the first try, the cow is on to you.

Hallowed be—how, it was my third try that day—how, and Three was on to us right away, anyway, even before the first try.

> So in one sense it is true that living within this frame pushes us to the closed perspective. . . . However, I have been arguing all along that the actual experience of living within Western modernity tends to awaken protest, resistances of various kinds.
>
> —Charles Taylor, *A Secular Age*

Hallowed be—how, I brought my guitar into the field—how, I sang hymns of comfort to Three—how, I called him by his Trinitarian name—how, I shared with him the songs that I want sung at my own funeral—how, each time he relented—how, he would be touched—how, he let me bat away the face flies that plague him.

Hallowed be—how, each time I prayed that you would help us get the cow onto the trailer—how, I reminded you that if we didn't get the cow on the trailer, there would be no meat for the people—how, perhaps if you miraculously got the cow onto the trailer, then maybe when you revealed yourself, Josh would believe again that you loved the world—or loved him, anyway—

Hallowed be—how, it was said, maybe in the *Odyssey*, that the bulls jumped themselves onto the sacrificial fires when the god in question was Zeus—how, I would have loved the romance of that or of a gentle good night.

> *"Enter through the narrow gate, for the gate is wide and the road is easy that leads to destruction, and there are many who take it. For the gate is narrow and the road is hard that leads to life, and there are few who find it."*
> —Matthew 7:13-14

Hallowed be—how, maybe you don't work that way? How, maybe 1 Corinthians 13 suggests that giving one's body to be burned for the glory of the story is maybe not what you're asking for?

Hallowed be—how, I couldn't think, even as I was moving the fence to that end, of any reason you should listen to my prayer and move Three toward his end—

Wattle

Hallowed be—how, I would have liked to have had the moral authority to remind you, if you needed reminding, for example, that you work vindication and justice for all who are oppressed and should therefore do x or y just thing—how, but in this case, it was sort of hard to see my personal hopes as "just"—how, because Three's not going on the trailer would mostly just cost us and our customers food, would be a humiliation—rookie, hipster farmers—but actually might be a sort of rescue of Three.

Hallowed be—how, and besides, Ramón might be lonely too, without Three there with him to flick a tail at the flies on Ramón's face—

Hallowed be—how, it dragged on for the whole thirsty day, moving fence, moving fence until the dark—how, it was like each time the mistake in the set-up was so tiny—this little gap, this small egress or moment of the fence made it not convincing—and he would approach the trailer and veer.

Hallowed be—how, he didn't believe in the fence—this break or that bit or height or step of the fence—how, Three sought and found the weaknesses, staked his bovine freedom on each breach.

Hallowed be—how, we went to bed with an empty trailer.

Lift up your heads, O gates!
　　and be lifted up, O ancient doors,
　　　that the King of glory may come in!
Who is this King of glory?

The LORD *of hosts,*
he is the King of glory. Selah

—Psalm 24:9–10

Hallowed be—how, we got up grim before it was light—how, it was just like when you know you're going to fail—how, but because you might not fail, you have to keep doing it anyway.

Hallowed be—how, it was our last chance—how, we moved the entire set-up to a different gate, a different part of the pasture—how, as if Three wouldn't know anymore what we were doing with that trailer—how, we thought that perhaps we could align the gate itself with the chute, for more stability—how, then we might convince the steer that the barrier was inviolable—how, it took us so long to set up, to pound in fence posts for the cattle panel chute—how, we weren't messing around, but raised up the cattle panels, roping them and carabinering them so that the chute fence was as tall as a person—how, we wired off, too, a third of the pasture, in a nonthreatening, gradual reduction of the field in a direction.

Hallowed be—how, we moved into the forest to roust them out—how, it was clear they'd not forgotten—how, I ran to the gate, to the trailer, ready to close the door—how, the steers then began a startled run down the chute—how, yes, it was working perfectly, and up came Three to the gate and I was going to swing the trailer door closed on him at last—how, I had it perfectly prepared

with slippery half hitches from camp—how, I had it un-
tied to push closed—how, our proximately increased ter-
ror at their massive size dissolved into Josh's desperation
and my singing and our utter weariness—

Hallowed be—how, then rose up the fierce will—how,
Three in his thunder—through the narrow chute.

> *The LORD has bared his holy arm*
> > *before the eyes of all the nations,*
> *and all the ends of the earth shall see*
> > *the salvation of our God.*

—Isaiah 52:10

Hallowed be—how, Three breached—how, not like
a humpback breaches—how, like Moby Dick breaches—
how, he leaped like a bull off the altar, over our perfectly
posted fence gate—how, he brought down whatever would
compel him—how, he crash-crushed the gate as he leapt—
how, he crumpled the dream of tidy order, its shifting
boundary lines and false freedom, for a season—how, he
felled the straight gate in his furious haste and emerged
unfazed, unhurt—how, he arced into the open field, tumbling full ecstatic, sublime as a bee for his full flower—

Hallowed be—how, promptly he nosed again at the
hospitable, considerate, expansive territory of grasses.

Hallowed be—how, Josh threw his hat into the field
in the unnumbing heat of the summer dawn—how, he
sat on the edge of the trailer, his head in his hands—

. . . the world becomes apprehensible as world, as cosmos,
in the measure in which it reveals itself as a sacred world.
　　　　—Mircea Eliade, *The Sacred and the Profane*

Hallowed be—how, Ramón and Three, placid as stilled waves under the command of divinity, noticed the hat in the grass—how, they sniff-nibbled it for a moment, nonplussed, then ambled their grazy way back to the forest to sleep, whatever the day's heat might bring.

Hallowed be—how, Three and Ramón, Ramón and Three, flick flies from each other's faces in the shade of the trees—how, maybe they sing to each other, but they do not sing for me.

We must once again endeavor, by adducing feelings akin
to them for the purpose of analogy or contrast, and by the
use of metaphor and symbolic expressions, to make the
states of mind we are investigating ring out, as it were,
of themselves.

　　　　—Rudolf Otto, *The Idea of the Holy*

Hallowed be—how, a window is a fence—how, a blind is a fence—how, a curtain is a fence—how, glasses are a fence—how, eyes are a fence—how, the whites of the eyes are a fence—how, a day is a fence—how, a dream is a fence—how, a flag is a fence—how, a family is a fence—how, a sentence is a fence, a jot is a fence, tittles are withies—how, a sign is a fence—how, a body—how, a woman's

body is a fence—how, an egg is a fence—how, a cracked
egg is a fence—how, a mask is a fence—how, that comment there is a fence—how, that rat cage round of perni-
cious thoughts spoken and unspoken is a fence—how, a
pandemic is a fence—how, a metaphor is a fence—how,
an amendment is a fence—how, a spire is a fence—how,
desires are a fence—how, I just want one nice thing is a
fence—how, a joke is a fence—how, a fence is a fence.

> *God has no satisfaction in reducing Isaiah to a gibbering*
> *mound of flesh on the floor. Bringing him to the point*
> *of realizing that he cannot even exist in the presence of*
> *God is not the purpose of the vision. Rather, that hor-*
> *rible realization is designed to prepare Isaiah to receive*
> *the purifying fire on his lips, which is in turn designed to*
> *prepare him for his mission.*
>
> —John Oswalt, *The Holy One of Israel*

Hallowed be—how, these leaning walls and tottering
fences.

> *I should have been too glad, I see—*
> *Too lifted—for the scant degree*
> *Of Life's penurious Round—*
> *My little Circuit would have shamed*
> *This new Circumference—have blamed—*
> *The homelier time behind.*
>
> —Emily Dickinson

Hallowed be—how, when that song by a nineties Christian band came on late Friday night—how, two teenagers were coming back from Beaver Camp—how, they pulled over the car and danced in the headlights right in the middle of the road at field's edge, because who else would be coming down Wright Street, late as it was—how, the fields slivered particular grass leaves around them in a full gleam of the silver light—how, summer in the Lord's presence—how, they were withies that would be.

Hallowed be—how, years later, when one of them tried that same worship dance in a rented living room, to a different tune—how, she slipped on the slick carpet—how, she broke her foot and missed the class on *Go Tell It on the Mountain*—how, she wore a hobble brace for weeks while it healed.

> *Still I kept waiting to* see *Jesus.*
> —Langston Hughes, *The Big Sea*

Hallowed be—how, just as I was weeding out the wattled garden, that mushroom hunter came up the driveway to say hello—how, he told me he has asthma, other diseases, but if it was God's time for him to go, it was fine—

Hallowed be—how, no less friendly, though—how, hiding what morels he'd found on the farm, of course—how, no less did he give me a dryad's saddle from his bag—

how, no less did he tell me how to cook its lemony sponge in butter—how, I did just that.

Hallowed be—how, it was the first stranger's face I'd seen in so long—the first whole body and face, his overalls, his pronounced limp—how, I see him glorious in that heat and light—how, the image of the Lord upon him—how, I believed him from within the fence—

And in this sodenly I saw the reed bloud rynnyng downe from under the garlande, hote and freyshely, plentuously and lively, right as it was in the tyme that the garland of thornes was pressed on his blessed head. . . . And full greatly was I a stonned for wonder and marvayle that I had that he that is so reverent and so dreadfull will be so homely with a synnfull creature liveing in this wretched flesh.

—Julian of Norwich, *Showings*

Hallowed be—how, when my son pulled the stabilizing fifty-eighth picket out for no reason—how, when he peeled the bark off the first post from some unfathomable, adolescent impulse, I cried—how, because why would you wreck someone's work like that—

Hallowed be—how, yes, I'm a little frail right now, who isn't?—how, but maybe it even seemed then that in order for you to show your arm, my own, tendons burning, would be broken.

Sanctity is not a matter of being less human, but more human. . . . The true saint is not one who has become convinced that he himself is holy, but one who is overwhelmed by the realization that God, and God alone, is holy. He is so awestruck with the reality of the divine holiness that he begins to see it everywhere. Eventually, he may be able to see it in himself too: but surely he will see it there last of all, because in himself he will continue to experience the nothingness, the pseudo reality, of egoism and sin. Yet even in the darkness of our disposition to evil shines the presence and the mercy of the divine Savior.

—Thomas Merton, *Life and Holiness*

Hallowed be—how, a fortnight later, he asked me what sandpaper did—how, I said it smoothed out the dents and digs—

Hallowed be—how, I saw him later that day, through a window, and he had snatched some sandpaper from a painting project I was working on—how, he was scraping it up and down the half-skinned, raggedy post—how, he did it as if secretly scratching smooth, up and down, "sor-ry," "sor-ry," "sor-ry."

Epilogue

*It couldn't have been for nothing that you wanted so many pages
of dimly lit, recondite things written: those forests of words have
stags native to them, who retire inward and revive themselves,
walking around and grazing, reclining and ruminating.*

—Augustine, *Confessions*, trans. Sarah Rudin

*One way to understand your own condition is to write something
and spend a long time revising it. The errors, the hits and misses,
the excess—erase them all.*

*Now read what you have rewritten out loud in front of some
other people. They will hear something that you didn't say aloud.
They will hear what was there before you began revising and even
before the words were written down. You won't hear anything but
the humming of your own vocal cords.*

—Fanny Howe, "Waters Wide"

Christ, have mercy

Acknowledgments

Invitations have always helped me so much as a writer, and this book would not have been written without the invitations of Mark Granquist, editor of the quarterly journal *Word & World*, whose out-of-the-blue welcome to the world of theology for ministry—and openness to formal oddity—provided the opportunity to make the attempts that became "Clearing" and "Wattle." I'm thankful also to Josh and Kerstin Mabie of Pied Beauty Farm, and to its matchless lyceum, for the invitation to share "Field" with such a kind and supportive audience: I was honored to carve my name in the podium. I appreciated, too, being able to talk out the basics of this book with Josh Mabie through some fourteen hours of conversation on a trip to a conference in Iowa—thank you for helping me see books as neighbors!

I'm so, so grateful to all who were willing to read my work and offer feedback, most especially Claude Atcho, Mark Clemens, Theon Hill, Miho Nonaka, Joel Sheesley,

Ally Stapleton, Nicole Mazzarella, Drew Bratcher, Tom Gardner, Rhonda Mawhood Lee, Craig Werner, Jenna Watson, Haleigh Olthoff, Jeffry Davis, Margaret Diddams, Chris Norton, Liuan Huska, Laura Yoder, Kristen Page, Lucy Henneker (what an inspiration your reading was!), and members of Wheaton College's Center for Applied Christian Ethics seminar on creatureliness. Many of the readers of this manuscript offered their feedback at great personal cost of time and attention—I am filled with wonder at the sacrifices that you made for me and this project. THANK YOU.

To the publishing team at Eerdmans, especially Lisa Ann Cockrel, William Hearn, Jenny Hoffman, Caroline Jansen, and Amy Kent. Thank you for your work and time on this project, your many kind and quick answers to my questions, and your willingness to welcome the weirdness of this book. I'm thankful, too, for the supportive and sensitive copyediting work of Victoria Jones.

I'm grateful for the encouragement of my writing group through its various phases and for Siobahn Carroll, Liz Ho, Ikram Masmoudi, Amy Wan, and Lilian Mina—as well as Stephanie Kerschbaum, who brought us together. They always understood the various farm crises that made my attendance spotty! And I'm always thankful for the support and care of the Village Tavern Scholars—Beth Felker Jones, Christina Bieber Lake, and Nicole Mazzarella. Yes, yes, every word out of my mouth *is* a cry for help—thanks for answering those cries and praying and laughing and sharing. Love and gratitude to Miho Nonaka and Becky Eggimann for the conversations that kept me going at some of the darkest moments.

I'm grateful to Wheaton College for the gift of a sabbatical on which to do some of this work—and for the willingness to let me work as a generalist and try new genres. Thanks to Wheaton College's Center for Faith and Innovation for support in writing "Forest," especially for the patience of Ben Norquist and Keith Johnson during the first panic of the pandemic. Thanks to Honey-Rock for providing the perfect retreat space to finish two chapter drafts: that Wellspring cabin is writing heaven! I'm particularly thankful to Ben Weber for the leisurely conversations and nerdery on *Piers Plowman*—to think of the hours we spent STANDING in the office doorway, marveling at the glory of that text and the bewildering resistance of some students to its wonders! If I still haven't got it here, don't give up on me, OK? That book takes a whole career to understand.

I'm grateful to my neighbors Geoff Martin, Mike Ello, and Arianna Trob Ortega—for helping us find wayward children and animals, for lawn mowing (and fixing lawn mowers!), and for friendship, and for repaying escaped-pig lawn damage with bags full of ripe crabapples for the wandering scamps. Thanks, too, to the various community members who have helped us woo back animals who have set their hearts on pilgrimage outside the edges of the farm, and to the Frontera Farmer Foundation for helping us with the infrastructure that will keep us persistent in the rotational grazing and silvopasturing that animals enjoy.

I'm exceedingly grateful to farmers, scientists, and environmental workers who have shared advice, help, knowledge, and encouragement with me over the years that ended up helping me in this book: Heather Whitney, Scott Hasselmann, Nena Hasselmann, Grama López, Grampa George Hasselmann, Mary Jane Schuring, Linda Balek, Cindy Crosby and her books and nature dinner club, Claire Hodge, Tage Shumway, Kristen Page, and most of all, of course, Josh Kriner.

I'm thankful for the prayers of many who supported this work: both those I know about and those I don't know about. I'm particularly thinking of Kathy Eberle and her team of North Country prayer warriors, as well as Elise Katter, Todd Katter, Corinne Kersey, Lee Cunningham Morgan, VTS, and Miho Nonaka.

Thank you to the Wheaton College English department senior seminar on land and story, with whom essential engagement with place and literature ideas were first worked out: Hannah Doan Morgan, Grace Gibbs, Valerie Griffin, Lisa Hemphill, Chloe Keene, Jake Krogh, Alley Lindner, Francesca Tso, and Charis Valmores Bootsma. My students in all classes have consistently helped me read my way into the place-based, conversational community in the love of the Trinity that has

Acknowledgments

fostered the meaning I long for. **THANK YOU**. Surely, *surely*, this is not without meaning.

I'm grateful to my family, especially my children, Fiona Kriner and Beckett Kriner, my parents, Joseph J. Eberle and Kathleen D. Eberle, and my brother-in-law, Jason Elliott, for helping at crucial periods with farmwork so that this project—and the farm! and my person!—could survive. Laying fence in ninety-five degrees in dense, prickly undergrowth, feeding an army of volunteers, painting the deck . . . the list goes on. Grateful for the conversations, support, and patience of Linda Kriner and Bob Kriner. Endlessly grateful for my siblings Kelly Clark, Becky Elliott, Kendra Eberle, and Joseph Eberle for encouragement, a working kitchen, and #twiceayear.

And to all volunteers at Root and Sky Farm—those Good Friday trenchers and tree planters, those sheep loaders, those bringers of encouragement and mercy and grape salad, those willing to make the trek out—may you flourish in your work, may blessings of root and sky be always upon you, and may more of you find your way here to partner with root and sky.

And to my husband and partner, Josh Kriner: I was walking in the fields the other day, trying to mow a perimeter for the cows with the push mower, thinking, wow—I get to walk here, see this, partner with all these created wonders. Who would have thought there would be so much love for the land, the animals, and the kingdom? It is undoubtedly all thanks to your very good farm dreams, your very hard work, and the very bewildering mercy of God.

I'm thankful for all those who've rooted in and cared for and paid attention to the land that this work considers, for ecological community building and husbandry through generations. I'm thankful to the animals and plants who have lived here, with whom I seek to partner.

And for your mercy, O Lord, I am most, most needy and most, most thankful.

Credits

Grateful acknowledgment is made for permission to quote from the following works.

The cover design of this book makes use of a detail from *Farm in the Snow*, a 1918 woodcut by Dutch artist Julie de Graag (1877–1924).

De Graag worked in a variety of forms and media: woodcuts, landscapes, still life paintings, portraits, botanical drawings, watercolors, ornamental illustrations, design work, and handwork. Her training at the Academy of Fine Arts in The Hague prepared her to render expressive, realistic detail, which precision her mature pieces selectively stylize. De Graag's expertly formed woodcuts, influenced by Art Nouveau, are marked by intense contrasts, but their intensity as much emerges from the works' profound sensitivity as the boldness of their forms. She also taught drawing and wrote a short treatise on embroidery design. A great deal of her early work was lost in a fire in 1908, but the works that remain evoke a sense of the emotional vitality of an artist who, encouraged by a community of fellow artists and mentors, continued to work despite health challenges and significant doubts about her own craft.